Praise for *Beyond Vengeance, Beyond Duality*

"Sylvia Clute does a remarkable job of providing a vision of hope and healing in the midst of enormous cruelty, injustice, and harm affecting millions of Americans—particularly those of color—caught up in our criminal justice system. Clute offers a much-needed perspective on our common human connection and the need for compassion, as well as accountability. *Beyond Vengeance, Beyond Duality* is a must read!"

—Mark Umbreit, PhD, Professor and Director of the Center for Restorative Justice & Peacemaking at the University of Minnesota and author of *Facing Violence: The Path of Restorative Justice & Dialogue*

"Ms. Clute's book shines a spotlight on fundamental flaws in the American approach to crime and the American criminal justice system."

—M. Gerald Schwartzbach, veteran defense attorney

"This compelling book offers us a new vision of not only our legal system and all its criminal and civil litigation black holes, but of our society—indeed, our world as a whole. In fact, that is the author's point—we need to see ourselves not as separate entities struggling for Darwinian-Newtonian dominance over and against each other, but rather as conjoined parts of a larger, more compassionate 'oneness' where the Golden Rule replaces 'an eye-for-an-eye.'"

—Fred Alan Wolf, PhD, author of *Dr. Quantum's Little Book of Big Ideas* and *Time Loops*

"Sylvia Clute speaks with the authority of experience in this compelling call for a holistic approach to justice in all its dimensions. Her book explores important distinctions: oneness v. duality, duality v. polarity, discernment v. judgment, power v. control. Restorative justice advocates will find it a fresh approach to the basic foundations of their field."

—Howard Zehr, Professor of Restorative Justice, Eastern Mennonite University

Also by Sylvia Clute

Destiny Unveiled, a novel about spiritual transformation
in an age of terrorism, war, and conflict.

www.DestinyUnveiled.com

A CALL FOR

A COMPASSIONATE

REVOLUTION

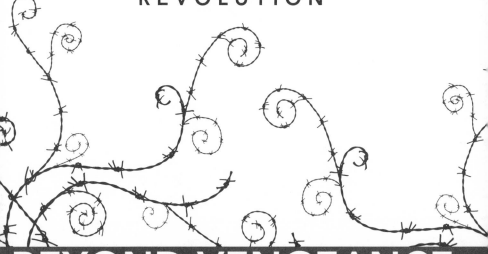

BEYOND VENGEANCE
BEYOND DUALITY

SYLVIA CLUTE

HAMPTON ROADS
PUBLISHING COMPANY, INC.

Cover design: Laura Beers
Cover illustrations: © iStockphoto.com
Text design: Donna Linden
Typeset in Avenir and Perpetua

Hampton Roads Publishing Company, Inc.
Charlottesville, VA 22906
www.hrpub.com

"Graph 1: The Punishing Decade: Number of Prison and Jail Inmates, 1910–2000"
reprinted with permission from the Justice Policy Institute.

Library of Congress Cataloging-in-Publication Data is available on request.
ISBN: 978-1-57174-633-7

Printed on acid-free paper in the United States of America
10 9 8 7 6 5 4 3 2 1
EB

To Sam, Mae, and Laina,
that their generation may inherit a better world,
then make it ever more peaceful.

Contents

Introduction   9

1   Becoming Our Own Jailers   13

2   What Do We Mean by *Justice?*   27

3   Two Forms of Justice   *38*

4   The Historical Roots of Justice   *48*

5   Root Causes: Oneness and Duality   *56*

6   Oneness: The Real Reality   *67*

7   Oneness and Religion   *75*

8   Science and Reality   *87*

9   Oneness and the Nation-State   *98*

10   The Language of Oneness and Duality   *111*

11   Institutionalized Oneness:
The Community Model in Corrections®   *124*

12   Institutionalized Duality:
The Stanford Prison Experiment   *133*

13   Practicing Oneness   *142*

14   Conditions Are Ripe for Change   *158*

15   A Compassionate Revolution   *171*

Appendix   *180*

Notes   *190*

Postscript   *199*

Introduction

When I entered law school in 1970, I was told I would be learning the best legal system in the world, an assertion that went unchallenged. There were still quotas for women and minorities, so my focus was on being as good, or better, than my male peers, the formula that had gotten me past the legal system's quotas.

The American legal system has deep roots in English Common Law, complete with its prejudices and shortcomings, as well as its strengths. For a couple of decades, I honed my skills as a trial attorney in this go-for-the-jugular, concede-nothing world in which the winner takes all. As time progressed it became clear that, win or lose, my clients were still estranged from their adversaries, and often the breach in their relationships had worsened. I began to doubt this was such a good system. Being a part of it became ever more difficult.

The conflict became intense when I realized that another system of justice exists, a form of justice that I rarely, if ever, experienced in the courtroom.[1] It works according to an internal design, matching perfectly with the circumstances being addressed— whatever they are. Equity and balance are integral to its process, enabling this system to embrace ever-changing possibilities without diminishing anyone's power. In this form of justice, all participants honor one another, enhancing harmony and goodwill in their interpersonal relations. Forgiving the past is mutually beneficial so that the present leads to a future free of anyone's bondage. Such justice emanates from love.

Eventually, my identity as a trial attorney and my internal moral compass formed a fork in the road. In 2003, no longer able to reconcile them, I stopped litigating. I realized that the form of justice I had been schooled in is fragmented, lacking in balance, and it precludes harmony. It was painful to realize how lacking the holistic approach to justice had been in my past training and experience as a trial attorney. Moreover, I realized we could have this alternative form of justice here and now because, when I knew what to look for, it was present in diverse places. It is found in some models of restorative justice, in transformative mediation, in certain religious teachings, in the Golden Rule, and even in what some call conscious capitalism.

I now call the two forms of justice unitive justice and punitive justice. We have all experienced both forms at one time or another. In this book, I share the story of how my struggle to understand the two distinct forms of justice eventually led to an unexpected realization. Each form of justice emanates from a distinct source: unitive justice emanates from the organizing principle of Oneness, while punitive justice is rooted in the disorganizing process of duality.

Oneness and duality are ancient concepts, but I had not previously understood their practical application in today's world. It is Oneness from which our perfectly ordered universe emanates, but the perceived chaos and pain of duality keeps us from recognizing the order that is always present. When we recognize that either Oneness or duality is at work, there is a constant and predictable order in everything. Through the lens of Oneness and duality, our world of greed, violence, and war in the midst of breathtaking acts of love, kindness, and generosity makes perfect sense.

While the language used may differ, many masters have taught that when we are in the mind-set of duality, we are blind to the Oneness that we share with all that is. When we are fully connected to Oneness, we see that duality is a state of mind dominated by fear expressed in its many forms, but that duality is a choice we need not make. Because we are created out of—and exist in the energy and consciousness of—Oneness, we can always access this under-lying, all-encompassing reality.

While this teaching has long been with us, what is different now is that the evolution of human consciousness is at a point that many of us can grasp its practical application to our material real-ity. As Oneness leads us to rediscover our lost sense of connection, we will naturally be guided to live in peace and harmony. What we need is a map to help chart the course of this historic journey. This book provides that map.

How can the old structures that are holding us back be trans-formed so this new order can unfold? How will a prospective change of this magnitude be received? Can we make the transfor-mation before it's too late? It's like standing on the edge of a cliff about to jump, not knowing if our new wings can carry us. The message that follows calls upon us to have faith—and to leap. We stand at a portal to the New World.

One

BECOMING OUR OWN JAILERS

It's time for systemwide change.

We live in a strange world. When an institution doesn't work, we prop it up over and over instead of fixing it, never seeing the dysfunctional patterns that imprison us. This strangeness encompasses many areas of endeavor, such as politics, religion, militarism, business, and finance. The U.S. criminal justice system is a prime example. After addressing crime by perpetually locking more people up, the United States now surpasses China, Russia, Iran, and South Africa in the proportion of our citizens behind bars.

More than one in every one hundred adults in America is in jail or prison.[2] In this land of liberty, our tax dollars pay to incarcerate one in every fifty-three of our young people in their twenties, at enormous cost to our citizens and loss to society. At the same time, college tuition is rising so fast, fewer and fewer young people can afford to attend. All the while, the rate of crime continues to increase or decrease, independent of how this system is used to control it.

When the costs are added up, every year an inmate spends in jail or prison costs us about the equivalent of one teacher's salary. We now have over 2.3 million people locked up on any given day, approximately the same number as China and Russia combined. That means a lot of teachers' salaries are being spent not on teaching kids but on locking up those kids' dads, moms, sisters, and brothers—and too often the kids themselves.

With 5 percent of the world's population, the United States now has more than 25 percent of the world's prisoners. This incarceration binge[3] is destroying the fabric of our communities, some more than others. One in every fifteen African American men lives in a prison or jail cell. If you are an African American male between the ages of twenty and thirty-four, the ratio is one in nine. Doing time is now so prevalent among young black men that, for many, it has become a rite of passage into manhood. One young man, the only male in his family who has not been to prison, told me he is chided for this failure.

Hispanics are disproportionately affected as well. As of 2006, one in thirty-six Hispanic adults was behind bars.[4] The resulting racial disparity affects our political process. Few states bar convicted felons from ever voting, but many mandate a period of years after release from jail or prison before reinstating voting rights. Kentucky, a state where the bar is permanent, prohibited almost 25 percent of its African American males from voting in 2008.

Men are roughly thirteen times more likely to be incarcerated than women, but the female inmate population is mushrooming. For black women in their mid to late thirties, the incarceration rate is one in 100. For white women, it is one in 355. Who is caring for the children of these women? What lessons is life teaching these kids, and how many teachers' salaries will those lessons cost us?

My husband shook his head. "This surely isn't true," he said, as we listened to these statistics recited on the evening news on February 28, 2008. *One in 100: Behind Bars in America 2008,* a report compiled by the Pew Center on the States, had just been released. Its sad findings also hit the front page of many papers and whirled around the Internet.

Why do I care? After all, many systems are in breakdown—the economy, education, and health care, to name a few. Perhaps it is because, as a trial attorney, I saw the problems in the legal system firsthand. I didn't handle criminal cases, but for twenty-eight years I tried civil cases where money, not freedom, was usually at stake. When I went to court to represent my clients, I often waited in the courtroom while the criminal docket was heard. There I got a glimpse of some of the inequities at play on the criminal law side. The judges were cordial enough to the defendants. "Sir, do you have money to hire an attorney?" they would ask penniless defendants, who were most often black. When the defendant said no, he would be assigned a court-appointed attorney.

Court-appointed attorneys, also called public defenders, are known for their work in ensuring that poor people get a fair shake in our complex criminal court system. Sometimes these attorneys work even when they are uncompensated for their time. In most cases, however, for the low fees they are paid, it is difficult to take all the measures needed to ensure their clients get the same degree of due process the wealthy can afford.

Before ever being judged guilty, many people held in jail (not prison) are awaiting trial. Those who can afford to post bail are generally released pending trial. Those who can't post bail remain locked up in what amounts to a modern debtor's prison. In 2006, more than 60 percent of those who spent time in jail were not convicted, a number that continues to grow.[5] Imagine the impact this has on their lives. Do they lose their jobs? What happens to their property? This not only impacts the lives of each of those individuals and their families, but it also unnecessarily increases the tax burden you and I must pay.

Politicians not only tout the criminal law system as the answer to crime, they also tell us it is the answer to a myriad of social problems, including homelessness, begging, truancy, runaways, and vandalism. It costs about eighty dollars per inmate per day to lock up people accused of things like turnstile jumping, Fish and Game violations, and dog leash violations.[6] If a person is cited for jaywalking and can't pay the fine, the penalty for nonpayment may well be a stint in jail. Some officials even demand zero tolerance to deal with behavioral problems in our schools, giving our children an early taste of how readily our culture uses punishment to secure compliance, foregoing other options.

Seeing retribution and greater vengeance as the solution, more acts have been classified as crimes, many prison sentences have become mandatory, as well as longer, and early release for good conduct has been all but eliminated. Judges are generally prevented from being lenient, even when the circumstances warrant it. This has led some defense attorneys to advise their clients to plead guilty to crimes they didn't commit, reasoning that a short sentence for a lesser crime is better than risking decades behind bars that would be mandated if convicted of a more serious offense. Rehabilitation programs, education, and training are targeted as soft on crime, scorned as treating the incarcerated better than those not involved in crime. At best, these safety nets are minimal.

In this strange world, prisons have taken up the slack for the state and county hospitals that released millions of mental patients between the 1950s and 1980s.[7] We were told that decentralized, neighborhood-based care was a better solution, especially since many more drugs had become available to aid treatment. The cheaper and more humane mental health and housing programs that were promised were never delivered. One reason was that we didn't want mentally ill people in our neighborhoods. Because the majority of people behind bars in the United States have some type of mental illness, our prisons and jails are our "new asylums."[8] In an effort to maintain control of systems gone haywire, some prisons now have mental wards.

When drugs and drug addiction escalated in the 1980s, we didn't examine the whole and assess the cause. Instead, the high-profile death of athlete Len Bias from a cocaine overdose in 1986, along with the growing use of crack cocaine, sent lawmakers on a spree to seek more retribution. They promised more punishment would finally produce compliance, but it hasn't.

The new laws dramatically increased the probability that a drug-related offense would result in a prison sentence rather than jail or probation. Prison sentences were made longer, especially for offenses involving crack cocaine, the cheaper version of cocaine which was prevalent in many black neighborhoods. Beginning in 1986, distribution of just five grams of crack carried a minimum five-year federal prison sentence. It took the distribution of five hundred grams of powder cocaine, one hundred times the quantity of crack cocaine, to get a five-year sentence. Before those mandatory minimums for crack went into effect, the average federal drug sentence for African Americans was 11 percent higher than for whites. Four years later, it was 49 percent higher.[9] The law has been changed, removing the sentencing disparity, but that is only a bandage.

As life sentences and sentences that span decades are now common, we have an expensive elderly prison population whose numbers are growing. Although criminal activity generally decreases dramatically with age, between 1992 and 2001, the number of state and federal inmates aged fifty or older almost doubled.[10] The elderly in prison can be easy prey for younger, stronger inmates. Hearing and visual impairments, incontinence, dietary intolerance, depression, and the early onset of chronic diseases like Alzheimer's, diabetes, or heart disease complicate the management of older inmates. The cost of keeping an older prisoner locked up is around seventy thousand dollars[11] a year or more—not one but two teachers' salaries.

Not everyone in the system is locked up for a long time. When you add up all the people who go in and out, about ten million cycle through our jails and prisons every year. They bring the lessons they've learned, the diseases they've contracted, and the trauma they've experienced back to our communities. While we like to think former inmates are the "other"—different and somehow separated from us—there is no wall between us and them. We are all in this together.

How much is this incarceration binge costing us? Nationally, our prison industrial complex, as it is now called, is a sixty-billion-dollar-a-year industry and surging.[12] Twenty years ago, all the states together (excluding federal expenditures) spent a total of 10.6 billion dollars on corrections. In 2007, they spent more than forty-four billion dollars—four times more in just one generation. During the same twenty-year period, inflation-adjusted spending on corrections rose 127 percent. In comparison, what we spend on higher education rose by only 21 percent.[13]

The increasing incarceration rate far exceeds increases in the rate of crime. During the newscast of the Pew Report, there was an interview with Kentucky governor Steve Beshear. He stated that in the last thirty years, his state's crime rate had increased about 3 percent, but its inmate population had increased by 600 percent. This is what our get-tough-on-crime policies have produced. Even our governors are trying to get our attention, letting us know that high crime is not the cause of our incarceration binge. These are the politicians who used to say, "Lock 'em all up," but not anymore.

Few people seem to consider what moral principles are driving these punitive policies, or their effect on the greater whole. The more money we spend on jails and prisons, the less we have for education, health care, and roads. If we fixed the criminal law system, we could save enough money to send young people to college for free, or at least at a low cost. This would be especially uplifting for those who otherwise could not afford it. Rather than saddle our youth with student loan debt, we would provide them with a bright future. So why doesn't this happen?

There are some who still contend that skyrocketing incarceration rates are responsible for keeping crime in check, but the evidence contradicts them. What's referred to as the New York Miracle—a sharp drop in homicides and violent crime rates in that city between 1992 and 1997—occurred when New York State had the nation's second-slowest rate of prison growth and when the city's jail system downsized.[14] San Diego is a city that reduced crime by nearly 37 percent between 1990 and 1995, and many attribute the reduction to the implementation of a neighborhood policing approach. The police began to share responsibility for identifying and solving crimes with the citizens and, simultaneously, the incidents of crime fell.[15]

Some countries that incarcerate prisoners for shorter terms have lower rates of crime. For the same crimes, American prisoners are locked up twice as long as English prisoners, three times as long as prisoners in Canada, four times as long as Dutch inmates, five to ten times as long as French prisoners, and five times as long as those in Sweden. These countries all have lower rates of violent crime than we do, and their rates of property crime are comparable to ours.[16] The argument that more punishment means less crime does not hold water. There are many factors that cause crime to rise and fall and, as we will see, punishment is not the only tool in our crime-reducing tool kit.

It's true, there are periods of escalating crime, and assuring the safety of our communities requires that some offenders—murderers, serial killers, psychopaths—be kept behind bars for long periods of time and perhaps for life. We have lost sight of the fact that these types of offenders are the exception.

Some states have applied bandages of various sorts to stem the tide of our broken criminal law system. Some hold lower-risk offenders accountable in less costly settings and use intermediate sanctions for parolees and probationers who violate the conditions of their release. Others use a mix of community-based programs, such as day reporting centers, treatment facilities, electronic monitoring systems, and community service. A few have even reduced prison terms for inmates who complete programs like substance abuse treatment, designed to cut their recidivism risk.[17] While these are helpful, they are not the systemic change that will lead to a solution.

When all is said and done, do we think we are safer? Decidedly not. Many of us still live in gated communities, arm our houses with security alarms, or sleep with a weapon nearby. Safety, security, and freedom have become increasingly rare commodities. We have become a nation of jailers, not only of petty offenders and serious criminals, but also of ourselves.

Who Are They?

Who are the people at the center of this misery, the ones behind bars? Each has a story that reflects our diversity and the entangled events of life. I got to know one of them, Daudi Beverly, when his mother called me for advice. She was desperately trying to find ways to help her son who was being swallowed up in a criminal system that she didn't understand but which she knew could destroy him. I didn't handle criminal cases, but her plea was one I couldn't refuse. I offered to walk with her through this process and, as I did, I saw firsthand how interwoven and complex the misery has become. Daudi has a lot to teach us about the depth of our systemic failure.

Daudi falls into that category of the one in nine black men between the ages of twenty and thirty-four whom we too easily forget. He is also one of the millions of the mentally ill, many released from state and county facilities in the 1950s–1980s, who represent the majority of people now behind bars in the United States.

According to Mary, Daudi's mother, he was a premature baby, born somewhat developmentally disabled. Mary is a strong woman with shiny dreadlocks down to her waist, the central pillar of her extensive family. Two of her children have master's degrees, and one is a teller in my local bank. Mary raised them well.

When Daudi was ten, his father was beaten to death during a weekend when Caribbean immigrants and drugs were targeted by the Washington, D.C., police. Mary was told that certain officers called such weekends a Caribbean cruise. She describes her former husband as deeply spiritual, a health-conscious vegetarian, and law abiding, just like she is. He wore dreadlocks as a symbol of wisdom and honor, to feel connected to his roots. He was not an immigrant and did not do drugs. But he was black, and his dreadlocks signaled to the police a questionable profile, based on common stereotypes. Mary reports that Daudi's dad and two other black men were beaten to death that weekend.

Daudi had been close to his father. He turned inward and refused to speak of his father's death. Within a few years, having lost the most important anchor and role model in his life, Daudi dropped out of school.

At age eighteen, Daudi was sexually assaulted by a leader of an African American church during a weekend outing. Mary was devastated. She had hoped the trip would be good for her son. Angry, hurt, and dealing with complex issues beyond his comprehension, Daudi threw a burning wooden penis into the leader's house. Though reacting as a traumatized child crying out for help, he was convicted of arson and joined the league of young black men with criminal records.

A year after the sexual assault, Daudi had his first psychotic episode and was hospitalized in a mental ward. Unable to afford private treatment, he received public mental health services and thereafter was repeatedly institutionalized by order of the officials.

As he struggled with life among the mentally ill, being retarded, and easily influenced by misguided peers, Daudi got into trouble. He was convicted of minor offenses such as trespassing, smoking marijuana, stealing a CD and potato chips, and car theft when the kids who had stolen the car left him alone in the vehicle.

Medications are critical to managing Daudi's illness, but many have negative side effects. It was several years before his treatment finally allowed him to at least perform yard work. Even then, Daudi found it difficult to remember directions or scheduled appointments with his therapist. Mary called repeatedly to help keep him on track. She says this seemed to annoy the mental health agency staff. Someone told her that because Daudi was an adult, she had no right to his medical information, so she should stop calling. Although he had been institutionalized in mental wards seven times, no one advised Mary that she could be named her son's legal guardian, and thus have a say in his treatment and care.

The system we set up to help people like Daudi continued to fail. After he missed several appointments, the agency closed Daudi's file for noncompliance, which cut off his medications. Daudi began to have psychotic spells.

On his twenty-fifth birthday, after he had been off his medications for months, Daudi was doing yard work for an elderly white woman. When she denied she owed him for his second day of work, saying she'd agreed to pay him for the overall job, not for each day, he reacted with anger. Feeling cheated, Daudi later returned to her house and demanded another day's pay. They argued. When he entered her house, she picked up a stick or a cane and hit him. He took the stick and beat her severely.

It was a traumatic and terrifying event for this old woman. Daudi was guilty and readily admitted he beat her up and took seventy-five dollars from her purse, which he felt was due him. His victim claimed he also took a diamond ring, but Daudi didn't mention a ring, causing Mary to wonder at the validity of the old woman's claim. This made a big difference in the criminal charges, because the value of the diamond made the robbery a felony instead of a misdemeanor.

Daudi was plagued by severe emotional problems and attempted suicide while he was being held in jail pending trial. The jail staff assumed Daudi was faking his distress and denied him access to mental health care or medication, despite the fact that the psychiatrist who examined Daudi found he was not mentally competent to stand trial.

After numerous episodes in jail, Mary pleaded that Daudi be seen by a doctor. He was put on medication, and his behavior became normal. He was then reexamined by the psychiatrist and found to be competent enough to be tried, although it appeared to Mary that no tests were administered.

Daudi's trial did not go well. He was represented by a court-appointed attorney who was paid about as much for the entire case as some private attorneys are paid for an hour or two of their time. I sat next to Mary during Daudi's trial, as a silent witness to the depth of her pain. Daudi pleaded guilty to two crimes: breaking and entering and robbery. He pleaded not guilty to the additional charge of aggravated malicious wounding on the basis that he had only committed the lesser crime of malicious wounding, not the aggravated version. This meant the prosecutor had to prove the more serious charge.

The prosecutor called the elderly woman's son to testify about the terrible beating his mother had suffered. Large blowups of her injuries were shown to the judge. Mary cringed at these and told me not a day had passed since the crime that she had not prayed for the woman Daudi had harmed.

Whether Daudi had committed aggravated malicious wounding or not was critical. The judge's decision hinged on the size of a scar on the woman's arm. I gathered from the testimony that, as a result of the attack, she could no longer live alone in her home. Yet it was the scar that would determine the more serious conviction. The woman's loss of independence was given little, if any, consideration. A criminal case is not about how best to heal the victim's wounds. It is about the state seeking retribution for its law having been broken, and there was no charge involving the woman's diminished quality of life.

No one testified on Daudi's behalf, not even the forensic psychiatrist who had found Daudi incompetent to stand trial and then reversed his position. That psychiatrist's testimony would have given the judge insight into Daudi's fragile mental condition.

I was upset by the failure of Daudi's attorney to present evidence regarding Daudi's lengthy mental history. His lack of access to medication at the time of the crime wasn't even mentioned.

After the trial, the police investigator who had handled Daudi's case approached Mary in the hall outside the courtroom. He told her that Daudi had always been courteous and was forthright about what had happened. She could be proud of her son, he said, apparently wanting to affirm that Daudi was not a ruthless criminal, as he had been portrayed.

Mary desperately wanted to tell the elderly white woman and her family how sorry she was that this tragic event had occurred. She wanted to apologize for the serious injuries her son had inflicted and for her inability to keep him on medication. Daudi also wanted to say he was sorry, but his attorney advised both of them to initiate no contact with the victim. Daudi's attorney probably feared a possible admission against interest—that his client would admit the truth and his own words would be used against him. In this adversarial format, if Mary reached out, that could easily be construed as harassment. Our punitive justice system rewards a skillful attack, but often stands in the way of attempts to reconcile.

When it was time for Daudi to be sentenced, the prosecutor asked that he be given twenty years due to the heinous nature of his crime, five more years than the maximum cited in the sentencing guidelines. Instead, the judge sentenced him to ninety years: fifty for the robbery and twenty each for the other two offenses, then suspended all but twenty-five. Since we have abolished parole, Daudi will serve twenty-five years at society's cost of one teacher's salary per year. Actually, inmates like Daudi who have mental disorders can cost more than that; in Daudi's case, the cost was contained by keeping him in isolation twenty-three hours a day.

After Daudi's conviction, I assisted Mary in being named Daudi's legal guardian, a civil matter I could handle. This enables the prison administrators to speak to her about his health care and, if he is ever released, she can see that he receives treatment. After being presented a summary of his medical history, the same judge who sentenced Daudi to what perhaps amounts to a life sentence, without hesitation, signed the order that said Daudi was not competent to manage his own affairs.

Some will see Daudi as solely responsible for his actions, saying this is just another black-on-white crime. But this is a story about all of us—our failure to care for one another, our desire for quick fixes and easy answers, and our silent acceptance of a seriously flawed system that extracts an enormous price. We pay financially, and we also pay with our humanity.

And yet, according to our complex system of criminal laws, "justice" was done. Daudi had his day in court: the state paid for his representation by counsel, the judge followed the rules of due process, and the victim got her say. But was justice satisfied in this case? Or does justice require more substance? In Daudi's case, and in the cases of many among the other 2.3 million like him who are behind bars, few people ask those questions.

Our dysfunctional patterns continue for decades, defended with the argument that we could do worse. The more meaningful question is, why aren't we doing better?

Two

WHAT DO WE MEAN BY *JUSTICE?*

*The legal system is not alone in causing deeply felt
pain and dysfunction. Many of us feel forced to choose between
what our inner voice tells us and what our job requires.*

One reason justice so often fails to produce the happy ending
we expect is because of the confusion about what the word *justice*
means. Does it mean impartiality? Fairness? Righteousness? Ren-
dering what is due? Getting even? Killing the wrongdoers? Forgiveness? Without a clear definition, it is possible for authority,
decorum, and technicalities to provide form masquerading as
substance, permitting us to conveniently mold the term *justice* to
justify the end we wish to achieve.

Our mixed beliefs about justice don't come solely from the
legal system. We learn such lessons many times each day without ever realizing it. Often in movies, on television. and in video
games, we see justice in the so-called good people attacking the
presumed bad people, not realizing the good people and the bad
people are doing the same thing—attacking and killing their enemies. The point is to make the bad people hurt as much as the
good people feel they have been hurt. A lose-lose situation for all
is deemed a win for the good.

When we declare "We want justice!" it is often coded language for a forceful attack, getting even, in which two wrongs are

needed to make things right. But those whom we harm often see us as guilty, in need of correction, or evil. In their eyes, the harm they inflict is justified. When they seek their next "win," another round of losing commences. We complain bitterly about the harm done by others, while justifying the harm done by us. It's as if we say, "Our killing is good; it's only theirs that is bad." When we fail to perceive as others perceive, how well equipped are we to judge their actions, especially when our own perception is clouded by vengeance, misunderstanding, or deceit?

When I entered law school in 1970, I commenced my training in what was described as the best legal system in the world. One exercise law students engage in is practicing legal arguments in what is called moot court. An especially memorable lesson about justice came when I first practiced my role as an attorney before a panel of moot court judges. As part of my argument, I allowed that there was some merit to my opponent's argument—because there was—but I contended that my client should win since the law was on our side. In the critique that followed, the chief judge shook his finger and said, "You never concede anything; you go for the jugular." Justice must be related to conceding nothing, I concluded.

When I opened my law practice, I endeavored to be a tough attorney, conceding nothing so my clients would win, which meant making their adversaries lose. When I was lucky, I was able to devise a shrewd attack that caught the opposing attorney off guard, thus enhancing our chances of winning. I built a successful practice this way.

Before I share some of my lessons learned in the legal system, it may be helpful to explain something that perhaps is not obvious. Our legal system can be viewed as having two primary functions. One function is to define how we are to order our relationships and guide our conduct in society. This is done through the passing of laws and regulations that set out the rules we are to follow. The other function comes into play when the first part is not working, when the rules are violated, crimes are committed, or people are hurt. Having the courts deal with such breakdowns is meant to keep people from resorting to self-help by taking the law into their own hands.

The part of the legal system that deals with how things are to operate works well. One example is the orderly processes we have for recording and transferring property ownership through sales, leases, wills, foreclosures, and a multitude of other ways. The laws and regulations for traffic control and safety at the local, state, and federal levels are another example, among many. This side of the legal system can rightfully serve as a model that other countries or cultures would do well to copy.

In the minds of many people, the part of the legal system that deals with breakdowns is where justice is dispensed. If a crime has been committed, the criminal courts handle the matter. In a dispute between individuals or business entities, the civil courts have jurisdiction.

My practice dealt with litigation among individuals in the civil division of the court system. As the judge or jury determines who is to blame and what will be done about it, giving the parties little say in the outcome, my first concern was telling my client's story as convincingly as possible. Building the best story is made respectable by calling it "the winning theory of the case." Clients would come in, describe the events that had led them to seek my help, and out of what they told me, I would select the facts that supported my winning theory. This usually meant presenting the story in a way that made my client appear to be the innocent or good person in the dispute, namely, the victim, and our adversary the guilty or bad one who had wrongfully victimized my client.

Ultimately, "the court chooses one story over the other in a win-lose ending,"[18] and this is called justice. This unique arrangement requires that trial attorneys be trained to be good storytellers, even when the facts make it an uphill battle. They must shape the facts to fit their story, and then minimize what is inconsistent.

Litigation replaced dueling with pistols, a self-help mode of resolving disputes. Neither was designed to make truth the primary concern. Although each witness is sworn to tell the truth, the truth is set aside when other considerations are more important. In fact, telling the truth about the heart of the case—whether you committed the wrong or not—is discouraged. As in Daudi's case, being truthful about a wrong you committed or a mistake you made is deemed an admission against interest. As such honesty helps the opponent and can be used to hasten one's defeat or increase the punishment, attorneys readily admonish their clients not to say things like "I'm sorry" or "I made a mistake." In criminal cases, the Fifth Amendment protects one from having to tell the truth if it is self-incriminating. To avoid costly blunders, the attorneys often control what is said by speaking for their clients. Few seem to recognize that a rule that punishes the realization and acceptance of personal responsibility destroys the trust necessary for all parties involved to heal and move on.

In this winner-takes-all system, the stakes are so high that the truth can easily become secondary to winning—for the clients as well as for the attorneys. Even when there is no intent to lie, defining the issues as a conflict to be won or lost makes it hard to see beyond this limited do-or-die perspective. Any common ground that may exist is discounted, for making a concession is to lose. Emphasis is often placed on a particular part of the story, a single act, or the last episode. Looking at a continuous, coherent picture is not built into the process, so the underlying cause of the dispute is rarely addressed. Our adversarial legal system often stands in the way of discovering the whole truth, and it was never designed to reconcile the parties.

In this litigation process, what does it mean to win? You usually get money, if you survive the appeals and can collect it. In some civil cases, the plaintiff is awarded a judgment that exceeds the total value of the defendant's assets, and still the person harmed is far from made whole. If you lose, at best you owe little; at worst you are deeply in debt. If you lose in a divorce, it can mean losing custody of children, losing a home or a business.

An attorney told me that once he objected to the testimony being offered by a witness in a divorce case on the grounds the witness was lying. The judge retorted, "This is a divorce suit. Everyone lies." When the stakes are as high as they are in cases involving families, we must expect people to rationalize that losing would be a greater injustice than telling a lie.

What is most important for many is being deemed right, whatever the cost. What some are willing to sacrifice to win in this system is sometimes startling. The children won in custody battles, for example, are often emotionally harmed by the process, and their rate of juvenile delinquency exceeds the norm.[19] Many jurisdictions have outlawed cockfighting, but what we do in custody litigation is sometimes not all that different. The fight begins, the blood spills, and the so-called winner gets the prize, all with little regard for the pain inflicted in the process.

Because the decision maker in this tug-of-war is a third party—a judge or jury rather than the parties themselves—dialogue and mutual consent are set aside as goals. Yet consider how unreliable judgment of another's acts can be in any situation. How many times have you judged another and later discovered you were wrong? How many more times were you wrong and didn't realize it? How many wrong decisions do our judges and juries make every day in courtrooms around the nation? It took a long time for me to ask myself if a judge or jury, hearing bits and pieces of contorted evidence, is the best way to judge guilt and innocence, much less make decisions about life and death.

About 130 death sentences have been commuted since 1973 because evidence later proved these people were innocent.[20] This alone is reason to think twice about how effectively our system separates truth from lies. Is the prosecutor's win more important than the truth about the guilt of the defendant? In many of these 130 cases, the answer was yes. Sam Millsap, a former Texas prosecutor, now speaks openly of having sent an innocent man to death by presenting weak evidence that later proved to be false.[21]

For years I didn't ask if this us-versus-them system was a good way to heal the underlying breach or dispute. That was not the intended goal. I was hired to win. Not only is the healing of wounds irrelevant, more wounding is often the result. My clients sought what the system offered, and for many years I did not know enough to ask if this was the model of justice they truly wanted.

When I intentionally presented evidence in court to make my client look good and the adversary look bad, I thought I was meeting my ethical duty to provide zealous representation. While some states have removed the zealous standard from their code of ethics, the underlying problem remains the same. Witnesses swear to tell the whole truth, but when this casts the client in a bad light, I faced a conflict the legal profession discretely overlooks—winning and the whole truth are at odds. Eventually I began to see that nothing I was trained to do helped address the underlying breach in their relationships. Instead, what I did made it worse.

Facing the Inconsistencies

Despite the competing currents and the mountain of rules about how to navigate these uncertain waters, I usually won my cases. When I did, it was easy to attribute the win to justice. When I lost, it caused me to reflect more deeply on what justice entails. Perhaps

I should explain that, being one of the earliest female attorneys to try civil cases in my city, when I began, all the judges were men. I often represented women in suits against men who were part of the establishment. For these clients, in that era, justice may have been an uphill battle from the start.

A case I handled in 1976, early in my career, involved a woman who was the deputy warden in charge of security at the maximum security prison in Richmond, Virginia, when she applied for the job of prison warden. She said that her superior in the Department of Corrections who interviewed her for the job, a man whom she had known for years, said to her, "Sue, you must think you don't need a penis to do this job." When a man with significantly fewer qualifications was given the job, she retained me to file a suit for sex discrimination in federal court.

At the trial, the man who had made the incriminating statement testified that my client had misunderstood. What he claimed he actually said was, "Sue, just think, you don't need a penis to do this job!" We won at the trial level, but lost on appeal. I could understand the logic used to reverse the lower court's decision, namely, that the Department of Corrections had broad discretion in who it could hire for this job. But how was I to tell my client that such logic was justice in her case? We both had our doubts.

In another case, one of my divorce cases, the husband was having affairs with several women. This made no difference in the way the trial court divided the marital property, even though the wife, my client, was a homemaker and had been placed in a precarious financial position by the divorce. The court held that the husband's infidelity was not a factor in deciding how the marital property was divided, because we had offered no evidence that the husband had spent marital funds on his various affairs.

Prior to this decision, I had seen many wives who were punished economically—denied alimony and property—because they were the guilty party in the marital breakdown. I had a hard time believing the court would have found no connection between fault and property division had the wife been the one who was having multiple affairs. To me, this looked like a biased decision. But like it or not, my client had to adjust her life to the ruling.

I handled two separate medical malpractice suits against the same doctor, a family practitioner who had a penchant for fondling the breasts of his female patients and calling it a thorough chest exam. Many women had complained about having been sexually violated by this doctor and the Board of Medicine had investigated him multiple times. These complaints had, with few exceptions, been routinely dismissed on the grounds that these women didn't understand all that a good physical exam involved.

In the first trial, the defendant's expert witness, also a practicing physician, was confident in his testimony about the innocence of the defendant. He described what a proper chest exam involved and assured the jury that was precisely what the defendant had done. We lost that case.

I felt the expert witness was an honest professional who believed the defendant had been subjected to a frivolous claim. I suspected he knew nothing about the many women who had previously filed complaints against the defendant. When I took the expert's discovery deposition in the second case, I had the records of the Board of Medicine available and reviewed each charge with him. He confirmed he had had no knowledge of any of the prior charges.

When this expert again testified on behalf of the defendant in the second trial, his testimony had a different tone. He testified that if there was any cupping of the breast that resembled fondling, that would be improper. This time we won. I credited it to the fact I had been thorough enough to inform the defendant's expert witness about the history of complaints, while the defendant's attorneys hoped to again keep this larger set of facts out of the equation. Does justice hinge on the attorneys' success at hiding their clients' faults, or bringing such faults to light? By this time, doubt had begun to creep into my mind about how much justice this system produced.

In my role as an attorney, a sexual abuse case that I handled in the 1990s caused me the most distress. I was representing a teen-age girl in a suit against her father, who had abused her over a pe-riod of years. The trial was several days away, and I was preparing my client to testify when she turned to me and said, "I don't want any of this. I just want my dad without the bad stuff going on."

I froze. What would happen to my contingent fee if she had her wish? Because I was paid only if her father lost and a money judgment was awarded to my client, I would lose my chance to be compensated for the hundred hours I had put into her case. As I realized how quickly my self-interest had come to the fore, something inside me reversed course. Our system is set up so that a conflict between the attorney and the client too often lurks in the background. With an unexpected turn of events, the attorney can stealthily choose who has to lose. The pageant of conflicts and hierarchies of winners and losers that I lived with for years paraded in my mind. After that case, walking into court never felt as good.

One of the last cases I tried involved alleged legal malpractice on the part of an attorney who had engaged in sex with his client. The attorney had represented the client in a federal sexual harass-ment suit against a former supervisor whom the client claimed had raped her. The night before the attorney and client were to appear in federal court for a settlement conference with the judge, they had worked late into the night in the attorney's conference room preparing for that meeting. The attorney and client ended up having sex on the attorney's conference room floor. The client was in treatment and on medication for various mental problems when the incident took place.

As the client's original sexual harassment case involved alleged sex with her supervisor, if the case went to trial, the client's sexual history was fair game for opposing counsel to explore. Her sexual history now included sex with her attorney. To say it was in the attorney's interest that the case settle is an understatement. At the settlement conference the morning after the sexual encounter, the attorney had pressured his client to settle. She did, but felt she did so under duress, and that she had not had a fair trial of her case against her former supervisor.

In the legal malpractice suit that I filed on her behalf against the attorney, the attorney admitted to having had sex with his client. He said she had forced him to do it, including oral sex, because he was afraid of what she would do if he refused—he thought that might have damaged her psyche even more. While preparing for the case, my client said any number of times she would feel much better if the attorney would just say he was sorry. In fact, a close friendship, more than a mere attorney-client relationship, had developed between them. Losing that connection left a wound that litigation could not heal.

As the trial judge announced his decision in favor of the attorney, he first acknowledged that what the attorney had done was worse than reprehensible. He explained that he was nonetheless ruling in favor of the attorney because having sex with his client was not what the attorney had been hired for. As the attorney had not been practicing law when he had sex with his client on his conference room floor, the attorney's outrageous actions did not constitute legal malpractice.

I knew such finely tuned, easily self-serving distinctions were not justice. With a heavy heart, I told my client we operate in a deeply flawed system. It is a fear-based, fragmented system of rigid mental concepts, often justified merely by virtue of the fact that this is how it has always been done. Separation among individuals and between communities is reinforced at every turn. Not only the court-defined guilty pay for this form of justice—we *all* pay. I no longer wanted to be a part of it.

A Broken System

In our system of institutionalized justice, people learn to accept justice as vengeance, unaware of the price they must pay to get what they want. The brokenness is widespread. Depression among attorneys exceeds that of any other profession, alcohol abuse is much higher than among the general population,[22] and the rate of suicide may also exceed that of any other profession or vocation.[23] Why would so many attorneys choose to take their life rather than continue to be part of this punitive model of justice? Being continuously forced to take stands that are counter to one's inner moral compass regarding healthy relationships makes for a highly unhappy work environment.

For a long time I practiced law without questioning the system's internal contradictions and inconsistencies. Eventually, I saw how the sense of prestige and power my legal career seemed to give me hid a deeper truth—that the win-lose approach in the courtroom causes everyone to lose in one way or another. Had they known it was possible, many of my clients would have preferred healing and restoration of their broken relationships over the vindication and revenge that the legal system offered them.

The legal system is not alone in causing deeply felt pain and dysfunction. Many of us feel forced to choose between what our inner voice tells us and what our job requires. Despite our efforts to keep it out of sight and out of mind, our financial structures, religious institutions, educational system, business practices, health care, and politics are all experiencing breakdown similar to that happening in the legal arena. When we look deeper, we start to see common elements that permeate the whole.

Three

TWO FORMS OF JUSTICE

When a breach in a relationship or the violation
of community norms occurs, we often fail to recognize
that we react in one of two distinct ways.

Americans are proud that they live in a nation governed by the rule
of law, as though this guarantees justice. Just what does the *rule of law*
mean? Does it merely refer to *form,* such as how the laws are established—by edict, order, or democratic vote, for example? Or does it
refer to the *substance* of the laws, the principles and goals, such as vengeance or love, that guide the policy makers who adopt the laws?

This is one of those terms that helps obscure the underlying
patterns. To say we are governed by the rule of law, in and of itself, is not enough. All 2.3 million people now behind bars in the
United States—one out of every one hundred adults in the nation—got there through the process we call the rule of law. Even
the ones who are innocent.

Substance versus form is an important distinction that touches
many areas of human endeavor. Confusing this distinction is one way
institutions fostering social dysfunction continue to survive. Discovering how this distinction has been glossed over by the legal profession in order to sustain the old structures provides clues to how this
has been achieved in other institutions. It is a common pattern.

We can use laws to legitimize both injustice and justice. There are many examples of the rule of law being used in misguided ways—Nazi Germany being one of the most egregious. The four allied nations prosecuted leading Nazis for war crimes in the Nuremberg trials following World War II (1945–1949), and this was seen as an important process in establishing the marked difference between them and us. We followed the rule of law in bringing them to justice.

As it turned out, a disturbing aspect of those trials was the fact that the defendants seemed not to be remarkably different from the rest of us, and they too were committed to the rule of law.

The Nazis tried at Nuremberg included fathers who loved their children and their wives. Some were practicing Christians; some had a quiet and unassuming nature, demonstrating that being an average person was no insurance against the commission of terrible crimes. They shared an allegiance to the ideological cause of making the world better by establishing a super race, one that emulated the Greek ideal of the human form. They were merely following group norms and obeying their inspiring leader. As the communal world we share is what shapes our identity, we can safely bet that none of the defendants saw themselves as evil or villainous.

Their means were barbarous, but in their minds, the end justified the means. Their devotion to the rule of law was what the Nazis relied on to keep them from appearing lawless and arbitrary. They did not murder or plunder without first passing a law or issuing an order that made it legal. They used the rule of law to whitewash their heinous deeds, while condemning to death those guilty of far less serious crimes, or no crimes at all.

Form—how the laws were adopted—trumped substance—the law's moral imperative and what it achieved. Unfortunately, form seems to have been enough to silence many of their would-be critics, permitting the widespread genocide to proceed. Was it necessary for us to portray them as monsters, evil to the core, for us—the good people standing in judgment—to reassure ourselves that our own transgressions could never be like theirs?

While the term *rule of law* brings to mind regulations instituted by governments, it is used to similar effect in many other places. Church doctrines, corporate policies, school rules, and cultural norms all serve as the rule of law in their respective contexts. When rules are broken and conflict occurs between individuals, among family members, within communities, and between nations, *justice* is what we commonly call the means used to re-establish the norms, enforce compliance, and maintain control. The governing authorities, whatever the setting, use the rule of law to legitimize their approach to justice.

When a breach in a relationship or the violation of community norms occurs, we often fail to recognize that we react in one of two distinct ways. On the one hand, our goal can be to punish the guilty. This type of justice seeks diminishment and the imposition of control to enforce compliance among those accused of violating the norms of the institution; its answer to harm is more harm. I call this *punitive justice*. Only after many years of honing my skills as a trial attorney in this go-for-the-jugular, concede-nothing world where the winner takes all did I recognize that there is another choice—a different type of justice.

This other system of justice is one that I rarely, if ever, experienced in the courtroom. It works according to an internal design that matches perfectly with the circumstances being addressed. As equity and balance are central to its process, it is capable of embracing ever-changing possibilities without diminishing anyone's power. All participants honor one another, enhancing harmony and goodwill in their interpersonal relations. Forgiving the past is mutually beneficial so that the present leads to a future free of anyone's bondage. Compassion and lovingkindness direct this form of justice, and the outcome is a benefit to all. I call this *unitive justice.*

I began to ask, what underlies such disparate results? Do these patterns appear beyond the issue of justice? However, what I was certain of is this: the rule of law can be used to implement punitive justice or unitive justice.[24] Whatever the context, be it a court-room or a family unit, a Fortune 500 business or a grade school, when we look beyond form, we must choose to achieve one type of justice or the other, for they are mutually exclusive.

Because ancient tradition and modern cultural norms have sanctioned both of these approaches to justice, we are given con-tradictory moral guidance. In one instance, we are told justice is found in proportional revenge: the old law of an eye for an eye, a tooth for a tooth. In the other, it is aligned with the ancient teach-ing we often call the Golden Rule: do unto others as you would have them do unto you. These conflicting moral codes reflect the two distinct forms of justice.

I realized we could have unitive justice here and now, even in our institutions, because, when I knew what to look for, it was present in diverse places. It is found in certain religious teachings, in some models of restorative justice, in transformative media-tion, and even in what some call conscious capitalism, as well as in other places I will describe later. Yet, the less functional model persists. What distinguishes these two paths?

Unitive Justice

The defining characteristic of unitive justice is its inclusiveness. Its goals are healing, restoration, and reconciliation, an approach aimed at producing relationships that are harmonious, equitable, and peaceful. This is not a new approach. Among aboriginal people on the continents of North America, Australia, and Africa, there were some who long ago found ways to hold an offender accountable in a community-based process that did not involve the humiliation, pain, deprivation, or alienation that characterize punitive justice.

As previously stated, unitive justice is grounded in the principle of doing to others what we would have others do unto us, a moral compass found in some form in every major religion and culture. As it is internal and ever present, this compass requires no consultation with experts, no reference to law books, or any reliance on religious dogmas. Quite naturally, it can guide us to meaningful accountability to the victim and the community, and often to forgiveness of the offender as well.

Being inclusive, unitive justice involves the participation of all who are affected in assessing the harm done and forging both a remedy and preventive measures, thus avoiding the separation that the us-versus-them system causes. Those harmed may include not only the primary victim, but also members of the victim's family, members of the offender's family, and the community at large. At the appropriate time and in a safe setting, the offender hears the victim and community members describe the harm from their perspectives. This furthers the offender's understanding and results in the moral learning that can motivate a desire to repair the harm and to be restored to the community. We saw heartfelt examples of this during the Truth and Reconciliation trials in South Africa after the abolition of apartheid.

Unitive justice approaches the victim and the offender as parts of a whole. Indeed, the well-being of the whole can only be measured by the well-being of each individual part. Thus, no one is forced to lose. The victim feels heard and valued, as the offender is held accountable in ways that are meaningful and aid the victim's healing, something mere punishment fails to do. Input from all involved, including the offender, about how to repair the harm contributes to a sense of fairness. The likelihood of further harm being done is reduced when the community supports the offender in meeting his obligations.

This process creates space for both forgiveness and remorse to emerge, and this leads to freedom for all. Freedom for the victim, because so long as a man believes he is a victim, he cannot love himself. Forgiveness relieves him of the victim role, and self-love emerges. It brings freedom for the offender through understanding that he too is worthy of self-love. We cannot love others while we hate ourselves.

As confidence grows in the capacity of the community to provide for the safety of its citizens through peaceful means, trust develops. The openness of this process facilitates reflection and introspection upon the whole system, including how the crime or breach arose and what we can do to avoid such breakdown in the future. Thus, only unitive justice has the power to restore balance and harmony among the victim, offender, and community, goals the punitive system does not address.

Beyond mutual respect, accountability, honesty, and integrity, we find that unitive justice has few rules that dictate how healing and reconciliation, harmony and balance, are to be achieved. Its internal design matches the circumstances being addressed, whatever they are.

Unitive justice appears to be the opposite of punitive justice, but it is not, so no struggle need occur for unitive justice to emerge. It finds within each conflict possibilities for healing and transformation. Retribution is inconsistent with its objectives and, in its presence, the perceived need for revenge withers. This is not mere idealism.

In October 2006, the Amish in Pennsylvania captured our attention after a man murdered five of their young schoolgirls and then killed himself. The people of this quiet community rushed to comfort the murderer's family and asked us to be forgiving. They showed us how, in extending lovingkindness in response to a wrong, everyone has an opportunity to find release and the possibility of transformation. The power embodied in their compassion stunned the nation. Many think we need swords to win, but it was their defenselessness that touched our hearts and brought honor upon their community as no sword could ever do.

Examples of unitive justice in institutional settings exist on a limited scale in some criminal law courts where restorative justice programs are implemented. It is found in certain schools and in some private organizations. Other examples will be described in chapters 13, 14, and 15.

Punitive Justice

Because punitive justice is most often the norm in modern culture, we are inclined to accept this response without asking whether it produces a value-added product or not. Let's stop to consider some of the substantive elements of this system wedded to vengeance.

Punitive justice is grounded in the belief in separation. We are fearful of those whom we see as separate from ourselves, and we believe our safety lies in controlling or defeating those whom we fear. This eye-for-an-eye model of justice takes retribution, revenge, and vindication for granted. It considers none of punishment's collateral damage that occurs within the larger community. Punitive justice fails to address how the infliction of further harm or the deprivation of liberty translates into taking responsibility or how it rights the wrong it seeks to address, beyond getting even.

Believing in separation gives rise to the notion of good versus evil. Punitive justice relies on a double moral standard tied to this divide that permits us to see the harm we cause as moral because we see ourselves as good, while the harm done by our enemies is immoral because we have deemed them evil. This dual morality permits us to project blame for our killing, for example, on those whom we kill, saying they are responsible for our harm because they are evil and deserve to die. As is often the case, when both sides view the other as evil, the killing becomes endless, while all claim self-righteous innocence. We fail to note that having two standards of morality—one for us and one for them—provides a flawed moral compass, even when matters of simple justice are at stake.

The so-called justice in the punitive approach is seen to lie in its requirement that the harm we do be proportional to the harm done to us. Under this constraint, we are to hurt those who have hurt us no more than we have been hurt—the balanced eye-for-an-eye approach. The scales of justice are an appropriate symbol for this system of proportional revenge. It reminds us that, in order to pass for justice, the gouged eyes and teeth knocked out by our side must be approximately equal in measure to the gouged eyes and teeth knocked out by our enemies.

While this form of justice requires a degree of restraint that definitely makes it superior to barbarism, it is far from the best we can do. Yet there are those who protest that anything short of punitive justice displays weakness or is soft on crime.

Unitive Justice Is Pragmatic and Predictable

Unitive justice does not condone or ignore wrongdoing. It is not a world of relative values or slack morals where anything goes. On the contrary, unitive justice reduces or eliminates wrongdoing by creating and maintaining a culture in which wrongdoing—by anyone—is not accepted behavior.

For example, in a prison in Virginia, when a guard ransacked an inmate's cell during an inspection, he was reprimanded. In the culture the warden has established and carefully tends, the cells of inmates are seen as the inmates' homes and are to be treated with the respect a person's home deserves. Inspections are to achieve their legitimate goal, not to violate the inmates' sense of security and self-respect that the warden is trying to instill. Misconduct among inmates in this particular prison is a rare occurrence. Being held to a common moral standard that applies to and benefits everyone motivates members of the community to measure up, accepting the organizing principle of the environment they are living in as their new norm.

Unitive justice is pragmatic and predictable. When shared community values do not sanction hurting one another—and this standard is applied to everyone—the need to use punishment to deter violence, to maintain order and control, quickly diminishes.

Some people object that the positive results of unitive justice take too long to produce. They prefer the quick compliance that punishment aims to achieve, not considering the time it takes to repair the further wounding and conflict that comes with it. The punishment-and-revenge approach does not restore harmony and balance within the community, and the control needed to constantly enforce compliance consumes many resources.

In contrast, unitive justice supports fundamental, enduring change and costs relatively little. Sometimes the time required to achieve monumental results seems to collapse as transformation occurs with lightning speed. This is actually relatively predictable in the right environment.

How the punitive model of justice has evolved—and kept the unitive form on the margins—is a story of missed opportunities and tragic choices. A brief overview of how we have come to this place is set out in the next chapter.

Following is a comparison of the characteristics and outcomes of each type of justice.

Punitive Justice	Unitive Justice
Harm done to others as punishment for harm done by them must be proportional.	Intentionally harming others is unacceptable by anyone under any circumstance.
It reflects the old rule of vengeance: an eye for an eye, a tooth for a tooth.	It reflects the old rule of lovingkindness: do unto others as you would have them do unto you.
Accountability achieved through suffering the punishment that is meted out by those authorized to do so by the law.	Accountability is achieved in ways that do not compound the harm to society and are meaningful to the victims.
The enforcement mechanism is the fear instilled by the authorities and the punishment they can inflict if you are caught.	The enforcement mechanism is an environment that holds all to a common moral standard and the incentive to be part of such a community.
It assumes punishment achieves compliance, while ignoring the collateral effects. Control must be endlessly enforced.	It assumes wholeness/interconnectedness is fundamental, and an innate desire to share such an environment exists in most people.
It is fragmented and does not look at the whole. (The inconsistencies would be apparent if the whole were examined.)	It examines single acts within the larger context to find lasting solutions that address root causes.
Winning is defined as making adversaries lose.	It assumes no one wins until everyone does.
Some killing is legal. Some killing is a crime. This line moves from time to time, depending on who is writing the law.	Killing is unacceptable, by anyone. When you attack another, you attack yourself in some way.
It is a dualistic legal theory in which people are divided between good and evil. The so-called good people's killing is deemed to be necessary, and therefore labeled moral.	In this world, all deserve to be treated with respect and dignity, even our professed enemies. How we treat others is a measure of our morality, not a measure of our enemies' sins.
Forgiveness is giving a bad person something that is not deserved. In this mind-set, the victim sees forgiveness as losing. No concession is made until the offender repents.	Forgiveness is seen as liberating the one harmed from negative feelings that are self-destructive. It creates space for true remorse to be experienced by the offender, and this promotes lasting second-order change.
The law is used to legitimize and legalize vengeance, revenge, retribution, torture, war— whatever force is seen as needed to secure compliance. This is a punitive system, and it makes for a punitive culture.	It sees in every wrong an opportunity to produce positive outcomes—the possibility of transformation for all involved. By assuring the health of individuals and communities, the nation's health is achieved.

Two Forms of Justice

Four

THE HISTORICAL ROOTS OF JUSTICE

Justice should be the solution to discord,
not the cause of more problems.

How our ancestors viewed justice, and how these beliefs have morphed and evolved over time, helps explain why we now view justice as we do. If we consider how we got here, we can more easily understand how a deeply flawed system has prevailed for so long, and why we have persistently failed to deal with the problems it presents.

Mishpat Versus *Hesed*

We are taught in diverse ways about justice, but such teachings are especially prevalent among institutionalized religions. It is no surprise that we find lessons about unitive justice and punitive justice in the Old and the New Testaments.

A distinguishing characteristic of Judaism has always been the sole sovereignty of God. For early Jews, physically attacking and defeating anyone who tried to impose their multiple images of God upon the Jewish people was seen as an essential duty. This punitive justice, called *mishpat,* justified accusation and condemnation based on guilt and unworthiness, a punitive model of justice that legitimized violence toward others.

However, also central to ancient Judaism was another concept of justice that relied upon love and steadfastness called *hesed*. The King James Version of the Bible translates references to this type of justice as "lovingkindness." This form of justice is unitive, as it requires one to care for the well-being of others. In the Book of Hosea, God responds to the people, "For I desire *hesed* and not sacrifice."[25] The biblical uses of *hesed* reveal that justice tempered by love is the standard by which all actions toward others are to be judged.[26] It mandates that acts of correction be motivated by the intent of restoring community and fostering Oneness, not diminishing them.

The conflict between these two views of justice is seen time and again. Mosaic law (i.e., dating from Moses) included humane regulations, such as the gleaning laws that benefited impoverished Naomi and Ruth when they arrived in Israel—an example of unitive justice. In the end, however, punitive justice became more prevalent in Western culture, often justified by the well-known passage from the Old Testament that sanctions proportional violence. The penalty for injuring anyone is to be injured in exactly the same way—fracture for fracture, eye for eye, tooth for tooth. Whatever anyone does to another shall be done to him.[27]

The mandate of proportionality reflected in the eye-for-an-eye measurement was, at the time, a step forward. By requiring that vengeance be measured by the brutality of the offense, proportionality instituted a measure of restraint, and was thus seen as being more just than what had preceded it.

The Code of Hammurabi, a collection of Babylonian laws developed during the reign of Hammurabi (ending circa 1750 BCE), codified this same eye-for-an-eye type of provision in what was called the *lex talionis*. This code institutionalized many earlier traditions, such as the brutal trial by ordeal, but was nonetheless an advance over earlier tribal custom in that it no longer permitted blood feud, private revenge, or marriage by capture.[28] Codifying the limitation of proportionality demonstrated a desire on the part of the ruler that punishment of wrongdoers be just.

How Our Justice Became Twisted

Modern criminal laws continue to reflect the belief that proportionality in the harm done constitutes justice. When people go to court, they learn this form of justice firsthand. Many take this lesson into other contexts in their lives, be it work, their church, temple, or mosque, or their home. More missed opportunities for unitive justice and tragic choices that have led us to this place are found in the roots of American law that grow out of English Common Law.

English colonists are largely responsible for the institutionalization of justice in the United States. However, their conception of the law had roots extending back to the Roman Empire, if not before. After an invasion in 43 CE by a large Roman army, the most desirable part of the British Isles came under Roman rule for a period of nearly four hundred years. During that period, the notion that justice was the domain of the ruler—and was not to interfere with his interests—became well established.

After Roman domination came to an end, the British Isles evolved their own distinctive law. With no strong centralized authority to maintain order, early English law became largely a local matter. While brutality was surely present, continued compliance and amicable relations provided an incentive to bring the community together to consider the matter and to seek compromise. Often judgments were rendered by the community, not by a presiding officer.

The loss of local autonomy began in the twelfth and thirteenth centuries when authorizations or *writs* issued by the king became widely used to restrict the jurisdiction of the local authorities. The writs eventually led to the establishment of the common law—law that was common to all of England,[29] and justice became the domain of the king.

It was at this time that a decision of enormous consequence was made, solidifying the punitive approach to justice. The king in essence declared that, when a crime was committed, the king would symbolically serve as the victim of the crime. Crime became framed as the breaking of *the king's law against murder,* for example, not as the actual killing of a person; or as violating *the law against larceny,* not as the loss to the person whose property was taken. In this way, the duty to seek vengeance and impose punishment fell to the king, and now, in more recent times, to the state.

This system that began centuries ago remains largely intact. This is why, in criminal courts today, cases are styled as *The Commonwealth of Virginia v. John Doe* or *The People of the State of Colorado v. Jane Doe* (i.e., the state acting as the people's agent).

When the charge is read, the statute that has been violated is always recited. The name of the victim may be mentioned to be more specific, but the victims' needs and community reconciliation have been rendered largely irrelevant. As the king took control, local communities lost their capacity to deal with conflict themselves.

Being confronted by the might of the state, if the accused lacks the financial resources of O. J. Simpson or Paris Hilton, it is he who now feels like the victim. Because this system pits the state's burden of proving guilt against the accused's right to thwart such proof, the victim's role is reduced to that of a mere witness for the state. This means defense counsel must try to make the victim appear as untruthful as possible. Caught in the middle of the attorneys' battle to win and make their adversary lose, the victim often feels revictimized.

The Chains of the Past

Basing the criminal law system on the king symbolically serving as the victim has resulted in a significant imbalance of resources for the accuser (the state) and the accused (the individual citizen). Making the king (now the state) the victim gave rise to many questions about fairness, so there were lots of rules designed to right the imbalance—or at least to preserve the appearance of fairness for the accused, even when substance was lacking.

Our rules relating to fairness between the state and the accused generally fall within what we call due process. These are legal rules designed to protect the individual against abuses by the state and include such protections as the right against unreasonable search and seizure, the right to a trial by a jury of one's peers, the right to be confronted by one's accusers, and the right to legal counsel. The provisions in the U.S. Bill of Rights were written primarily to constrain the might of the state in its roles as accuser, prosecutor, and punisher.

As justice is seen to hinge on the state proving its case pursuant to the intricate rules of due process, the presumption of the accused's innocence trumps truth, transparency, and trust. Even guilty defendants are encouraged to plead not guilty, the rules often permit or promote nondisclosure of relevant facts, and suspicion of the other side is normal. Crimes become case files that must be expeditiously processed through the system, for the system's legitimacy depends in part on the speed with which judgment is imposed.

At no point does the punitive system use or teach the skills needed to create a harmonious civil society. Moreover, local wisdom about community conditions that promote crime and how to involve families, schools, and neighborhoods in crime prevention is lost. Many view onlookers' nonresponse to a crime as a lack of care or concern. In fact, it is more likely a reflection of the long-term exclusion of these citizens from any role in addressing local crime or the conditions that promote it. On the contrary, they are told to leave it to be dealt with by those with legal authority, even when moral authority is lacking.

A process that addresses the offender's individual accountability to the victim and the community is replaced with state and national institutions that rely on state-inflicted punishment, force, and retribution to maintain a tolerable level of compliance. Communities shackled with heightened separation and fear are a consequence. The voices of forgiveness and remorse that underpin unitive justice are silenced, making all of us—collectively and as a culture—victims of this punitive process.

What we have, instead, is an intricate web of laws developed over the centuries that is often woven of abstract concepts unconnected to the truth. Our law books are full of them, like whether the case is proven by a preponderance of the evidence, or by clear and convincing evidence, or beyond a reasonable doubt. My measure of these concepts and your measure may be quite different, depending on what we consider important.

What do these rules actually mean? After twenty-eight years of trial work, I came to this conclusion: They acknowledge that, in the punitive model of justice, we are forced to devise rules to guess at the truth and to inflict punishment even when the truth is unknown. Constraining vengeance by some measure of proportionality, these rules preserve the appearance of seeking retribution in a systematic, seemingly civilized way.

Punitive justice uses control and forced compliance to masquerade as order, but it is tenuous at best. On occasion, we see a bit of mercy, but the laws come from a place of fear and have little to do with compassion or loving one another. The decorum of the courtroom, its trappings of authority, and the might to enforce the rulings handed down tend to deter us from asking probing questions about simple fairness and reason.

Justice should be the solution to discord, not the cause of more problems. This is what unitive justice can achieve, one person at a time, making one choice at a time, as we look to systemwide change. What is lacking is political will on the part of our policy makers—and spiritual will on the part of our religious leaders—to make unitive justice the norm. This will change as our cultural assumptions about the value of punishment evolve and our lost sense of connection reemerges.

A Better Way

In Western culture, the eye-for-an-eye measure of justice went relatively unchallenged until Jesus of Nazareth did so, as reported in the New Testament. In the Sermon on the Mount, Jesus demanded that this old law be replaced with a new covenant that says: do not resist violence; love your enemies; pray for those who persecute you; when slapped on one cheek, turn the other cheek. To many, these were radical concepts, but necessary for consistency in the morality taught by Jesus.

He taught that the real world exists in living in equal relationships with others, not in controlling them; in loving your neighbor as yourself, not in getting even; in doing unto others as you would have them do unto you, not as they have done. Those to whom Jesus ministered were the most oppressed and tyrannized by the Roman authorities, but his teachings gave them hope. Why? Because Jesus taught that there is another way of being in the world, that justice does not depend on the empire's revenge and death.

Jesus forced into the open a comparison of justice grounded in lovingkindness and that of proportional revenge. This means each time a conflict is dealt with, there are two extrinsic norms at opposite ends of that spectrum by which to measure the morality of one's response: the extent to which the mode of justice chosen aligns with an eye for an eye or the Sermon on the Mount, with violence or nonviolence, with fear or with lovingkindness. When the Golden Rule is the preferred moral standard, punitive justice loses its legitimacy—its flaws are unmasked. Thus, Christ's challenge to punitive justice threatened the established order.

As was to be expected, the message of Jesus met stiff resistance. The vastness of Rome's control over what is now Western Europe, the Middle East, and North Africa was achieved and maintained using violence and repression. Because some strict Jewish religious sects used punishment, even execution, to enforce their particular restrictions, rituals, and observances, the teachings of Jesus were a threat to those sects as well. In Jesus' case, the state and ultraconservative religious orders shared a common interest in his demise. His was a message they feared and suppressed.

The teachings of Jesus have inspired millions over the centuries. But even as Christianity spread, punitive justice prevailed. Many who followed in the footsteps of Jesus saw his world of love through the eyes of fear and distorted or marginalized his teachings of nonviolence. They thought they had to preserve vengeful justice; it was what they knew, and their institutional structures depended on it.

There are moments in history when a fork in the road is encountered and a choice of monumental proportions presents itself. For the Western world, the teachings of Jesus presented an opportunity of this magnitude—and still do.[30]

Judaism and Christianity are far from the only religions to teach that justice can mean both vengeance and lovingkindness. Many religions have doctrines that legitimize punitive justice. At the same time, every major religion has teachings that support unitive justice. In the next chapter we begin to see how these contradictory messages reflect an underlying order that explains how we repeatedly choose conflict and misery; it also reveals how we can choose peace and harmony instead.

Five

ROOT CAUSES: ONENESS AND DUALITY

Most of us respond in remarkably consistent ways to our environment, which is inevitably built upon one of two distinct thought systems. One supports happiness, and the other promotes misery.

Why do we continue in our ineffective, often destructive, patterns? It is as though we have learned the code of misery and routinely apply it without thinking, always hoping it will lead to happiness. It never does. Why haven't we found the code to happiness? A lot of background noise keeps us from imagining it is within reach.

We are so accustomed to the status quo that we think this is how it has to be. Old institutions are tenacious, and they have long tentacles rooted in history and in a multitude of choices made by our ancestors. Law, history, religion, science, and culture all play a role in keeping us entrenched in dysfunctional structures. In ways we often fail to recognize, our parents, teachers, and public officials persuade us to accept the status quo, even when it is damaging.

Simply put, there are two distinct thought systems that underpin unitive justice and punitive justice, and they apply far beyond the question of how to respond to a breach in relationships or what happens in a courtroom. These two approaches to how we see the world guide how we, as a nation, distribute our resources and view health care, national defense, education, and the environment. They shape the philosophies by which we, as individuals, run our businesses and raise our children.

The Larger Context: Oneness and Duality

Every human activity is founded either on the organizing principle of Oneness or the disorganizing process of duality. There are marked differences between them. The organizing principle of Oneness encompasses the whole, while the disorganizing process of duality is enmeshed in separation and fragmentation. One leads us to harmony and healing, the other to discord and disease.

Oneness and duality each have their own set of rules and underlying assumptions about human nature, and even about the nature of God, a topic explored in chapter 7. Pro-social norms reflect the principle of Oneness; anti-social norms reflect the process of duality.

The Golden Rule, when it means more than merely doing good to others to deter them from doing bad to you, is a moral standard that is consistent with Oneness. In this context, others are seen as being of inherently equal value, and therefore deserving of equal treatment. An eye for an eye and its sanction of proportional revenge, on the other hand, comports with duality. Those at the top must control those at the bottom.

When we activate the organizing principle of Oneness, we are expressing our cocreative function as both spiritual and physical beings, conferred upon us by our all-encompassing, benevolent Source—what many people call God. When acting in accordance with the disorganizing process of duality, we have lost touch with our God-given nature, what some call the fall from grace. The underlying disorder is obscured from view by the morass of entangled beliefs and doctrines, perceptions, and emotions that preoccupies us.

Oneness can go unrecognized, but it cannot be destroyed. It is what is. Oneness applies to everything and everyone. Only Oneness is real. We have no need to learn Oneness, because internally we already know—it is who and what we are. We need only wake up to our truth and leave our dualistic misperceptions behind.

Oneness and duality are nonphysical structures that operate beyond the material realm and yet are present within it. We experience the vibrational pattern of duality in the body as the well-known sensation of fear. It manifests as vengeance, hate, greed, jealousy, anger, arrogance, judgment, guilt, shame, and the like—feelings that denote separation. When we feel fear, we shut down in survival mode and build institutions to protect us against our enemies.

We experience the vibrational pattern of Oneness as sensations in the body that we recognize as love, which can be expressed as gratitude, generosity, compassion, hope, trust, inspiration, harmony, joy, forgiveness—feelings that reflect our connectedness. When we feel love, we feel nurtured and we heal and grow; we build institutions that support healing and growth.

I digress a moment to address the hot button that the word *love* may set off in some readers. *Love* is a word that has been so often misused that its meaning has become distorted. We find that some in the legal community who engage in punitive approaches use the term in one context or another to describe their motives and actions. There are those who reject its use by the religious community because they have seen it used to facilitate manipulation or control. Another complaint is that counselors too often encourage their clients to bury their grievances and call that love, instead of achieving the second-order change that comes with transformation. Some scientists reject the word *love* as not being real enough. Others object because they see it as a sissy word that denotes weakness.

The concept of unconditional, pure love is not one we can afford to forego, and there is no satisfactory term to use in its place. As the concept of love is critical to a discussion about Oneness, I will use the word *love,* but ask the reader to set aside past prejudices, understanding that I mean love in its purest form—lovingkindness[31] and the true connectedness from which harmony and peace naturally flow.

Oneness and duality are like two separate containers. The container of Oneness can hold certain human experiences, such as trust, transparency, generosity, reconciliation, forgiveness, healing, restoration, faith, hope, compassion, security, and peace. The container of duality holds different experiences—suspicion, secrecy, divisiveness, judgment, attack, revenge, retribution, greed, jealousy, insecurity, and war. Any aspect of life can be constrained within the small container of duality, or it can be transformed to reflect the all-inclusive container of Oneness.

It is important that Oneness and duality not be mistaken for paired opposites, one good and one bad. Duality is not even real. It is a projection by minds blind to their Source in Oneness. Our blinded minds accept institutionalized duality, like a system of laws that imprisons one out of every one hundred adults, or military drones that permit killing without having to experience the humanity of the lives extinguished by the touch of a button, or usurious interest rates that concentrate wealth in the hands of a shrinking minority, while thinking it's generous to use our empty churches on off days to provide just enough services to the homeless to make homelessness doable. We were not given the gift of life to live so callously.

The Organizing Principle of Oneness	The Disorganizing Process of Duality
Oneness works according to an internal design, matching perfectly with the circumstances being addressed—whatever they are. It is circular, holographic—not linear—in nature.	Duality is fragmented; separation is paramount. Everything is seen as opposites locked in conflict, divided. Reality is seen as linear, making neat divisions possible and separation seem real.
Everything is interconnected; inclusiveness is central. The world is a field of energy in which everything is interwoven. What happens at one place in the field affects the entire field. My thoughts thunder through the universe, determining what I create.	Nothing is seen as interconnected. The world is made of matter separated by empty space. What happens in one place is seen as unrelated to other parts of the whole. My thoughts and deeds are seen as unrelated to the whole.
Equality can be recognized only in Oneness, as equality implies an inclusiveness that does not exist in duality. Where do we find such equality and inclusiveness? In the Golden Rule, for example, or in the command, "Love others as I have loved you." These permit no exceptions.	Inequality rules. Top-down hierarchies, status, social strata, castes, exclusive enclaves; it is us versus them at every turn. Judgment is pervasive, although those who cast the stones are often no better, sometimes worse, than those at whom the stones are thrown.
Oneness's moral imperative takes the form of monomorality. The same standard must be applied to others as you apply to yourself, such as in the Golden Rule. Equality is inherent in this standard.	Duality's measure of morality must be dualistic for the disorganizing process of duality to work. Our measure of morality and the measure we apply to others are different.
The organizing principle of Oneness is activated through the emotion of love, in all of its many forms, such as kindness, generosity, abundance, joy, forgiveness, trust, transparency, etc.	The disorganizing process of duality is activated through the emotion of fear, in all of its many forms, such as anger, greed, jealousy, suspicion, secrecy, scarcity, attack, etc.
Problems are addressed by considering the whole, as the whole is where the problem exists and the solution is to be found. Seeing how everything is interconnected, root causes can be identified and addressed, making solutions long lasting and cost effective.	Problems are blamed on limited causes, often what or who is most conveniently accused. The whole cannot be considered, or the insanity of duality would be apparent. Therefore, problems persist, and their "solutions" are expensive and ineffective.

Beyond Vengeance, Beyond Duality

Duality

As we consider the familiar world of duality in greater detail, let's begin with what duality is not. Duality is not polarity. On the Earth plane, polarity is found in night and day, male and female, black and white, acid and alkaline, among many other examples. The opposites in polarity are objective facts generally accepted by everyone. So long as we live in physical bodies, polarity is integral to the experience.

Duality's opposites, on the other hand—good and bad, pretty and ugly—are subjective projections and judgments. Confusion between duality and polarity causes us to misunderstand the nature of good and evil. We tend to think that good and evil are like night and day, but they are judgments; one person's judgment about who or what is evil may be widely disputed by others. Good versus evil is an example of duality, not polarity.

The disorganizing process of duality is a fragmented mental structure. Its predominant characteristic is the endless categories of what seem to be opposites locked in competition or conflict, like insiders versus outsiders, Catholics versus Protestants, Muslims versus Jews, Luke Skywalker versus Darth Vader, and on and on. These perceived opposites give rise to endless divides between pretty-ugly, winner-loser, strong-weak, and the like. Our minds become trained to think in terms of hierarchies, and our language becomes distorted, structured in such a way that judgments and projections are mistaken for reality, and fear is confused with awe and veneration.

When duality is activated, a pervasive belief in separation is inevitable, and fear is the overriding emotion. The perception of fear causes the body's cells, including the brain cells, to shift into survival mode, focused only on the perceived threat. Everything but this narrow band of perception is blocked out. As the cells are locked down in survival mode, they cannot grow or regenerate, making our persistent fear a slow march toward disease and death.

Attack—mental, emotional, and physical—is the reaction to fear and the modus operandi for dealing with the so-called enemy. The need to attack is not questioned, only whether to do it now or later. These attacks are considered moral because the enemy provokes them and is blamed for what we do. This leads to thinking that harming others is a win, necessary to keep oneself from being harmed, which would be a loss. Thus, even killing others can be called a victory.

Attack is sanctioned, of course, only when done by those authorized to impose control. Parents can spank, the state can kill, nations can annihilate, while certain others are punished when they attack. As no consistent logic is involved, who is punished for attacking is inconsistent and frequently unpredictable, producing distorted, meaningless results. No explanation we would want to hold up to scrutiny explains the disproportionate number of poor blacks and Hispanics locked up behind bars is one example.

Duality and the physical world are inseparable. In the dualistic mind-set, the material realm is experienced as a place of constant lack. The fear of material scarcity affects everything—beliefs about how much money, physical beauty, or the number of physical possessions one needs to have. Driven by fear, we strive to satisfy our cravings and the impulse to possess what we do not have by ensuring that others get less. Grasping and greediness, hoarding and scheming are coping mechanisms to deal with the driving fear that exists because, no matter how much one has, it is never enough.

Immediate wants must be satisfied. Responsibility for duality's destructive consequences is shunned, and the cost is forced upon others who receive no benefit. Take the coal plant owners, for example, who maximize their profit by minimizing their accountability for the pollution their plant generates, while their employees suffer health problems or their neighbors' property values diminish.

In duality consciousness, individuals see themselves as better or lesser than others, resulting in a hierarchy that mirrors the layers of fear. There is no common source that unites everyone within this system. Only fear is shared by all, but this commonality produces no bonds because its sources are as numerous as those who experience it.

When fear is the problem, it cannot be cured by all the material possessions in the world. It's like trying to mend a broken heart by sticking a bandage on your chest. As fear is a mental structure that provokes an emotional reaction in the body that tells us a threat is present, it must be healed at the point of the fracture—the mental structure. Thus, only love can heal fear, as love's mental structure fills the body with the sensations that arise in the presence of lovingkindness, telling us all is well.

We err in thinking that those who harm us are fundamentally different from us. Most of us respond in remarkably consistent ways to our environment, which is inevitably built upon one of these two distinct thought systems. One supports happiness, and the other promotes misery.

Duality at Work

We find the fragmentation that duality requires throughout the system of state-sponsored punitive justice that was described in chapter 1. In the criminal law system, for example, the police determine who is stopped and questioned. The prosecutor or grand jury decides who is charged with which crimes. The trial judge or jury determines guilt and measures out the requisite degree of punishment. After the judgment is rendered, the judge may assume that he sends those whom he has judged to a place of redemption, where their so-called lesson will be learned, but he has little control over that.

Like the others, the warden and executioner are also free of responsibility—even when an innocent person is wrongfully incarcerated or, worse yet, executed. After all, they had no part in laying the judgment of guilt upon those convicted.

Because authority for these acts is attributed to "the people," personal liability is rare for any missteps along the way. Each official acts as an isolated agent of the system with limited accountability for his own part, much less the whole. This enables everyone involved to overlook her own mistakes, see them as singular events, and ignore their cumulative effect. No one is responsible for the whole, even when it is broken. Actually, many do not realize the whole has become fragmented and unworkable. Balance, harmony, and equity are unachievable in this context, so they are viewed as unrealistic ideals.

Law is not alone in reflecting duality. One of the hallmarks of organized religion is its fragmentation. When a feud or misunderstanding arises within a denomination or a church, starting a new one is a common reaction; when this happens, duality is at work. There are now thousands of separate denominations in the United States alone. Many of us join religious institutions that are set up to be hierarchical, distinctly separate, and competitive, giving little or no thought to how this contradicts teachings about love and forgiveness.

Government is no stranger to duality. Only in duality could a political system exist that uses the manipulation of the peoples' fears as a tool to govern, or violence as a means to keep social order. If we were to look at the whole, it would reveal the flaws inherent throughout the system, so the whole must be ignored. Anyone who draws attention to the brokenness is branded as a traitor or an outsider, not to be trusted, too idealistic, or unpatriotic. Us versus them must prevail.

This fragmentation is not without its benefits to certain people. Those who want to maintain control can use the fear of their subjects to manipulate them, keeping them focused on one threat today and another tomorrow.

The fragmented structure of duality can exist only as long as we entertain the belief that this chaotic world of separation is rational. The adherents of duality call it realism; its opposite is viewed as optimistic fantasy and wishful thinking. But in duality, what is truth differs from one person to another, from one episode to the next. How can this be reality? The only way such a subjective reality can exist is if we are each projecting our own beliefs and our inner reality upon the outer world. This win-lose mind-set keeps us from grasping the mind's potential for wholeness and harmony.

Duality distorts who and what we are; to know only duality is to know very little. We live in a perfectly ordered universe, but because disharmony, imbalance, and disunity permeate duality thinking, we cannot see the order that lies beneath the perceived disorder. Duality is costly and destructive, wasteful of resources. In its fragmentation and fear, peace is unachievable. Duality leads first to conflict, then to war, as we ratchet up the force required to achieve submission.

Duality seems to be real because its fragmented construction restricts awareness to only that which conforms to its distorted view of reality. This leads to a world of distorted perceptions that must constantly be defended because they are fabricated, and not reality. Withdraw the belief that duality is real and it is exposed as dysfunctional, wasteful, and a recipe for ever-present fear, pain, and disaster.

While this pervasive mind-set of negativity is not reflective of the truth about the whole, we needn't look far to determine that duality is the norm. It permeates many systems, not only law, religion, and government. In this mind-set, we think it is rational to run our businesses as top-down hierarchies, setting them up so management and employees compete for scarce resources. Our emphasis on competition can be healthy fun, but it can also become cutthroat, each competitor for herself, bent on winning at any cost. Many families live in the unhappy reality of duality every day, one faction or member projecting negativity toward another as a way of life, often for the slightest of causes.

However, while duality is difficult, it contains a paradoxical blessing. For some, when they hit bottom, the painful consequences of duality make it easier to embrace the Oneness that has always been present.

Six

ONENESS: THE REAL REALITY

Just as a mathematician would not expect to arrive at a correct an-
swer without including all elements in an equation, when applying
the principle of Oneness, answers to problems are sought by first con-
sidering all relevant elements of the whole.

Oneness seems a world away from duality, in large part because the perception of separation disappears. We must not mistake Oneness and duality for polarities, nor are they opposites. In Oneness, everything is understood to be unified, like a giant container for all that is, including the pain and misery of duality. It provides the context in which we choose our path—Oneness or duality—in the exercise of free will.

Oneness is like the ocean and duality the wave. A tidal wave of duality can be destroying a small part of life while at the same time the ocean of Oneness is sustaining vast reaches of life, assuring it continues without ceasing.

Oneness is the path to peace, for those who comprehend the organizing principle of Oneness understand that to harm another is to harm themselves. This does not mean the tit-for-tat harm that duality sanctions, but rather is reflected, for example, in the deteriorating effect the emotion of hate has on the mind and body of the person experiencing the hate, or in the slave master's loss of freedom to maintain the enslaved. In fact, if I hate another person,

I will be harmed, but whether the person I hate is harmed by how I feel depends on whether she joins in my projection and makes it her truth. Likewise, the slave may experience more freedom than the slave master. It is a choice.

Oneness is characterized by balance, harmony, and equity. It is a system with no losers; it is understood that no one wins until everyone does. If we want to be healthy, it is in our interest that others be healthy. If we want to be safe, our goal must be to make others safe. What makes them safe—be it nuclear disarmament, safe drinking water, or low crime rates—makes us safe. We want to contribute to the well-being of others, knowing that adds to our well-being. We achieve enlightened mutuality in seeing our interests aligned with the interests of others.

Oneness reveals that the contrast between good and evil is like a mirage; it depends on where one is standing, the lay of the land, the temperature, not on what is true. *Evil* is the term used for those whom we perceive as separate from ourselves—our enemies—when we are operating in the realm of duality. When engaging in this process, we call upon its dual standard of morality to deem our attacks legitimate and good. When we enlarge our field of understanding, we see that evil arises when there is a broken link to Oneness. When we look deeply enough, we find that harmful acts are a cry to be reconnected.

In truth, what appears to be different is more like a mirror, reflecting one's own weaknesses. When one looks deeper, the *other* is a holographic reverberation of one's own self. A simple example is the fact that we often hate in others those traits that reflect our own flaws; we attract to ourselves that which we spurn.

Just as a mathematician would not expect to arrive at a correct answer without including all elements in an equation, when applying the principle of Oneness, answers to problems are sought by first considering all relevant elements of the whole. We then see how a multitude of pieces weaves the larger whole and can get at root causes. In wholeness we find solutions to problems that otherwise seem entrenched. In fact, solutions based on Oneness are effective, long lasting, and cost far less than fragmented ones.

Oneness embraces transparency, knowing there are no secrets because there is nothing light cannot illuminate. In fact, no matter how hard we try, what secrets can ever be kept? Not Monica Lewinsky, torture at Abu Ghraib, or Valerie Plame's covert CIA identity. Not even the silent thoughts we hold can be kept a secret, for they are reflected in the patterns of our lives. Our intent that we want to keep private is seen in the outcome we produce. In Oneness, this is not a problem, for there is no incentive to hide or distort the facts when everyone understands that their interests are fundamentally the same as those with whom they are dealing. This honesty leads to the trust that is characteristic of Oneness.

As we become more adept at activating Oneness, the body plays a different role. It is the vehicle for us to be in the world, but not of it. It is our means of experiencing happiness and joy. The dualistic beliefs that undermine good health, often held unconsciously—we don't deserve to be healthy, or by succumbing to disease we can punish those whom we love who have hurt us—disappear. Good health becomes easy and natural.

Equality

The quest for equality has been elusive, but it comports perfectly with Oneness. Equality implies an inclusiveness that allows no exceptions. It therefore cannot exist in duality, for the separation, hierarchies, and judgment of duality are intended to exclude. When equality is tied to the material world, measured by what one has or does not have, it suggests a form of equality some would not even find desirable, much less achievable. Mother Teresa would not have wanted the material affluence of Imelda Marcos.

It is interesting that we find the inclusiveness necessary for equality in some of the most universal concepts taught by major religions, such as do unto others as you would have them do unto you, "love one another as I have loved you,"[32] and love your enemies. These permit no exceptions. While it may still seem like this is not achievable, the community model program described in chapter 11 is an institutional model that incorporates this concept of equality.

The inclusiveness found in equality is also present in the recognition that we each possess an inner radiance beyond our humanity. We are created in the image of God, as the Bible states, and thus, each of us is equipped to serve as a secondary agent of creation by expressing love on the individual/physical level. We must recognize this power belongs to *everyone in equal measure,* for any exception to a universal principle negates the principle. At the same time, we can each inappropriately use the creative agency we are endowed with by lapsing into fear and clouding the truth with our misperceptions.

This is where free will comes into play. We each possess free will, and we must choose to act as agents of creation or miscreation. Total willingness is essential to the experience of Oneness—love must be freely given. Moreover, individual will is the factor without which the continued evolution of higher stages of consciousness on the subjective plane cannot unfold. The organizing principle of Oneness is the structure within which this occurs.

Do unto others as you would have them do unto you is the overarching moral law found in Oneness, precisely because it treats all equally. As we choose how we are going to respond to what we perceive, the Golden Rule admonishes us to perceive our neighbors and ourselves as equal in value, thus worthy of equal treatment—for our own good. From our perception of ourselves as created in God's image, we perceive others to be made in God's image, and naturally do unto others and ourselves in equal measure. All benefit.

From the perspective of duality, it, of course, seems like this is not achievable, and too risky to even be desirable. When we look from a broader perspective as we do in later chapters, experience shows that it is imperative.

The Consistency of Oneness

The organizing principle of Oneness is universal and consistent. As reason would predict, its universal nature means no one is exempt, whether one is aware of the principle or ignorant of it. Unintentionally living in harmony with Oneness produces positive results just as surely as when one intentionally does so. Unintentionally activating duality is just as certain to result in misery as intentionally doing so. We can only apply one moral standard at a time and, like it or not, the one we apply to others comes full circle and shapes the world we experience. Oneness applies uniformly to all; it makes no exception in favor of anyone; inclusiveness and equality are inherent throughout.

Those who have activated duality do not escape the principle of Oneness. Take giving and receiving, for example—what you give, you get. When we give a person something good, we are not surprised to receive something good in return. Oneness assures, however, that even in duality, giving and receiving are one. People who want to harm those who have harmed them share duality with their enemies, including its separation and pain. Those who secure compliance or the defeat of others by projecting fear and attacking them must be experiencing fear and attack in some form themselves for this to be possible. For those who have activated Oneness, projecting fear and attack is not part of the experience.

Those shrouded in duality cannot comprehend Oneness. The laws they rely on are marked by the separation and fragmentation that characterize duality. Even the rules they declare have been dictated by God are inconsistent and fragmented. In their dualistic mind-set, God's laws are seen as multiple rules and regulations that require specific knowledge and intent to comply with them, such as how one must be baptized or what position to be in when praying. Compliance with these laws is signified by following specific forms—rites, rituals, and traditions—that separate adherents from non-adherents, those who share the covenant from those who do not.

To Catholics, God's law might demand that no meat be eaten on Fridays during Lent or that priests be celibate. To Protestants, God's law might demand that they not dance or drink alcohol. These are just a couple examples among many religious rules that apply only to selective groups or that have changed with time. These are laws made by humans. Such inconsistency has nothing to do with the all-encompassing law of Oneness. Its law is eternal, not limited by time, place, or practice.

When we activate Oneness, we experience peace, harmony, and joy—the natural outcome of being an expression of love in the physical realm. It then becomes apparent that, when we activate duality, our fearful images of the world keep us from expressing love and ensure that we experience more fear. Choosing duality is to experience a world where contradiction reigns and opposites make endless war. Oneness ends duality's contradictions.

Laws written by humans, be they members of a legislative body, a body of clerics, or a lone school principal, are also governed by the principle of Oneness. When our laws operate according to the process of duality, as punitive justice does, we cannot escape the misery they inflict, the only question being, how and when are we to also suffer? Unitive justice is an example of human law that is in harmony with Oneness. All who experience it benefit.

The Order of Life

When we order our lives around Oneness, we see that duality is a mental structure dominated by fear expressed in its many forms, but that duality is a choice we need not make. Because the organizing principle of Oneness is universal, we can always access this underlying, all-encompassing reality. Evidence of the all-encompassing nature of Oneness is found in the fact that in every negative event lie the seeds of transformation and rebirth. When the whole is taken into consideration, duality's projections, judgments, and separation are seen as a mistaken understanding of reality. They are a painful path that some choose to take on the journey toward Oneness, not outside of its inclusive embrace.

Spiritual masters of all the major world religions have taught how to achieve Oneness, but it is by no means the exclusive domain of religion. Oneness is taught as a way of life in diverse cultures, such as the African way of Ubuntu. This is how Archbishop Desmond Tutu describes Ubuntu:

> It is the essence of being human. It speaks of the fact that my humanity is caught up and is inextricably bound up in yours. I am human because I belong. It speaks about wholeness, it speaks about compassion. A person with Ubuntu is welcoming, hospitable, warm and generous, willing to share. Such people are open and available to others, willing to be vulnerable, affirming of others, do not feel threatened that others are able and good, for they have a proper self-assurance that comes from knowing that they belong in a greater whole. They know that they are diminished when others are humiliated, diminished when others are oppressed, diminished when others are treated as if they were less than who they are. The quality of Ubuntu gives

people resilience, enabling them to survive and emerge still human despite all efforts to dehumanize them.[33]

Through the lens of Oneness and duality, our world of greed, violence, and war in the midst of breathtaking acts of love, kindness, and generosity makes perfect sense. This knowledge enables us to make better choices, intentionally activating the organizing principle of Oneness by acting from a place of love, not fear. As we awaken to Oneness as reality, a better, more peaceful, world is assured.

Seven

ONENESS AND RELIGION

Despite religion's ancient ties to Oneness, duality remains a competing, and often prevailing, governing principle.

Oneness, duality, and religion have a long history, one that has played a central role in our understanding of what is moral and just, and even what is real. Religion warrants more in-depth consideration.

It is undeniable that religion, despite its many positive influences, has contributed to its share of misery on Earth. Take my case, for example. I grew up in the midst of what I call the religious wars. My mother's family was Old Order Brethren. My father's mother was Irish Catholic; my paternal grandfather was nonreligious. Both sides of the family were upset when my parents married; their interdenominational marriage violated both family codes.

The two sides of my family rarely got together, and when they did, fights quickly broke out over who was going to Hell the fastest. The Brethren believed that to go to Heaven, you had to be fully immersed three times, facedown, when you were baptized. The Catholics believed a few sprinkles of water by a priest were enough. Though they were all Christians, in their allegiance to conflicting religious dogmas, the two sides of my family destroyed the essence of Christ's teachings—they couldn't break bread together.

It was hard to make sense of their feud. When visiting my mother's family on the plains of Kansas, I saw they were good, honest, hardworking people who strongly desired that their children have a better life than they had known. My extended Catholic family was centered in my small hometown in Colorado where most of my Irish Catholic grandmother's ten brothers and sisters lived. They were no different. With so much in common, I wondered why they couldn't get along.

I came to see how widespread these fundamental similarities were when, in my early twenties, I served as a Peace Corps volunteer in a remote village in Nepal. I lived among Hindus and Buddhists and found that the Nepalese, whatever their religion, were no different from my family in the States. They too were good, honest, hardworking people, and their children were paramount in their lives.

My childhood religious experience was the source of many of my beliefs, though not always the ones the church intended. I was raised Catholic, and in grade school I attended summer catechism classes where I memorized lists of the cardinal sins that would send me directly to Hell, and the venial sins that would cause me to take a detour to Heaven via Purgatory.

I recall bursting into tears one morning when the nun told us that touching the Communion host was a cardinal sin that carried the ultimate punishment. The host was a small, dry wafer that always stuck on the top of my mouth, so I would pry it loose with my finger. In response to my flood of tears over my innocent transgression, the nun told me I might not go to Hell after all. This was my introduction to doctrinal loopholes.

Doctrinal loopholes are used to deal with the inconsistencies that plague religious teachings that apply the disorganizing process of duality. But religious teachings that apply the organizing principle of Oneness need no such loopholes.

Religion's Ties to Oneness

From ancient times, teachings about the transcendent, unified One-ness—by whatever name, be it God, Allah, the Void, Source—have been fundamental to every major religious tradition. Inscribed on the ancient Egyptian temples were the words *nuk pu nuk,* meaning "I Am That I Am." *I Am* is an announcement of the Absolute, before the existence of the material realm, before any extension into space, and before the bounds of time—the infinite and eternal. The organizing principle of Oneness is a manifestation in our realm of this transcendent, unified Oneness.

At the time of the ancient Egyptian mystery schools, the masses were not expected to understand this truth about all that is. Its meaning was shared only with those few initiated into the great mysteries of Osiris, while the masses were occupied with rites and rituals, magic and myth. But as organized religion spread over the millennia, the ancient secret of Oneness became general knowledge taught to all believers. Today all major theistic religions have as a central teaching on the concept that God is One, the all-encompassing Source of which humans and nature are aspects or expressions.

For example, Hinduism, the world's oldest major religion, teaches there is one all-pervasive, transcendent reality that dwells in the hearts of all beings. In this tradition, it is called Brahman, the Absolute. The Absolute appears as many deities, or faces of God, that teach diversity is an attribute of God. According to Hindu philosophy, the truth is One, but different sages have given it different names.

In the Hebrew tradition, the opening words of Genesis tell the story of creation, of one Creator, leading to the conclusion that the originating principle in all things can be nothing but God or Spirit as Source. The Oneness of God is affirmed in the sixth chapter of Deuteronomy, "Hear, O Israel; the Lord our God is one Lord." Sharing what the voice of God teaches, Isaiah declares: "I am God and there is none else."[34] When Moses encounters the burning bush, God says to him, "I Am That I Am."[35]

When Jesus was asked to identify the greatest commandment of the Jewish law, he replied, "The Lord is One."[36] For Christians, this is the first of all commandments, and Jesus said he came not to destroy the law but to fulfill it.[37] The apostle Paul also spoke of Oneness when he taught that, in God, we all "live and move and have our being."[38]

The central message of Islam is that there is one and only one God, and that God is single and unique (*tawhid*). The first half of the Muslim testament of faith states: "There is no God but God." Islam teaches that the primary duty of humanity is to remember that there is only one God in all one's thoughts, words, and actions (*dhikr*).

While many Buddhists embrace the concept of a unifying reality, Buddhism does not emphasize being a believer in God or other transcendent power. The Middle Way of Buddha is one of balance and harmony—attributes found only in Oneness—but the focus is on practice, not on ideas and beliefs. To the Buddhist, there is one reality which need not be called God.

Those of the Bahá'í faith believe in a single eternal God, who has created all the creatures and forces in the universe. Spiritual traditions embraced by tribal cultures, such as Native Americans and Australian Aborigines, are also based on the belief in the Oneness of all that is. Although people have different concepts of God and God's nature, and call God by different names, all-encompassing Oneness is a widely shared belief among the world's religions.

From these teachings, we are able to comprehend the organizing principle of Oneness; it is a reflection of the Oneness of God, as expressed on the level of our spiritual and material existence. Of course, one does not need to be religious to comprehend Oneness. Many agnostics and atheists would likely agree that certain universal principles apply to all of humanity. This leads to the question, where did these principles come from? If we simply follow the chain of probable events back in time, we ultimately reach one unified Source, the universal First Cause.

Despite religion's ancient ties to Oneness, duality remains a competing, and often prevailing, governing principle. For example, certain religious doctrines teach us that the nature of God is consistent with the organizing principle of Oneness, but doctrines that link God to the disorganizing process of duality often hold greater sway. Doctrines that teach us about the nature of humanity contain the same contradictions. Ultimately, we cannot make sense of our chaotic world or ourselves without addressing these inconsistent religious teachings, and how some run counter to Oneness.

The Two Natures of God

Despite widely shared beliefs in one unified Source that many call God, this is not the only image of God that is found in the teachings of organized religion. In one lesson about the nature of God, we learn that God is omnipotent, omniscient, and omnipresent and we are told anything less would not deserve to be called God.

In another lesson, we are taught that what is called evil is a force in and of itself that can overwhelm us in our weak moments, and that some people are totally possessed of evil. In this lesson we learn that God is not present where evil exists. Most often, there is no lesson about how these two concepts of God are contradictory and both cannot be true. Thus, religion plays an important role in sustaining the belief that Oneness *and* the fragmented world of duality are both real.

However, if God is omnipresent—present everywhere—and God is not evil, then evil cannot exist beyond our judgment and projections. For a principle to be universal, it can have no exceptions. If

God is omnipotent—all-powerful—then evil can have no power over us, for God's omnipotence negates that possibility. If God is omniscient—all-knowing—then evil is not a separate intelligence that plots or snares. This consistency in the nature of God gives logical order to the concept of a loving God and other theological teachings about love and forgiveness.

Duality's image of God, on the other hand, is fragmented. It cannot be omnipresent, for where evil exists, this God is not present. As there is an evil intelligence or mind outside of this image of God, it cannot be omniscient—all-knowing. This God cannot be omnipotent, because an evil force exists beyond it. This image of God is consistent with the fragmented mental process of duality.

Duality relies on this splintered understanding of God for good versus evil to be considered a rational system, but where would evil get the control over God that this system attributes to it? Not from God, for no diminution of life can come from an omnipotent God that manifests only as love. Only minds shrouded in duality could dream of a God that must yield to evil.

This is the God that commands us to be fearful, and even vengeful. Inconsistencies are explained away by the image of a wrathful God who punishes sinners by condemning them to Hell. Using a wrathful God as our model, we are taught that good people have a right, even a duty, to punish bad people. When terrible things happen that can't be blamed directly on evil people, they are blamed on God's wrath, retribution for someone's sins. Even when these sins are not our own, we cannot escape.

Duality's pattern of violence answered by more violence mirrors its image of God. Only in worshiping duality's God, constantly locked in a battle with evil, could we fashion a remedy for harm done that involves hurting others, and then excuse our own harmful acts as moral. Only in duality can there be war between "my God" and "your God." Indeed, only in duality can there be war.

The loving God of Oneness, however, does not punish, for this is not what the innocent deserve; we are taught, instead, to rejoice when a wayward son comes home. By discerning when someone chooses to act contrary to love, we can respond in ways that support them in choosing to change their actions in favor of love. This is why unitive justice is the only justice; it stops the harmful act and then allows what God has created to emerge and be affirmed.

Understanding God from the perspective of Oneness leads us to see that our fear-based attributes—dual morality, vengeance, greed, violence, control, secrecy, and all the rest—are not the opposite of love, but rather distorted expressions of it. They merely reflect our choice to let duality's God be our master, instead of using our free will to express God's love in this physical world, as children of God are meant to do. The fallen angel, Lucifer, is a metaphor for our choices, not God's. When God is again understood through the eyes of Oneness, subservience to duality's God will simply end.

The Nature of Man

The two conflicting views about God inform basic assumptions about humankind, where we again find opposing images tied either to Oneness or duality. It is a prevalent religious belief that humans, like God, have two contradictory natures.

First, we are taught that humanity is created in the image of God, a view consistent with Oneness. This lesson says that we are the subjective and individual reproduction of the all-encompassing origin of creation, even while we are physical beings. Many religions teach that God is love, meaning that the knowable presence of God in our physical realm is love, expressed in a multitude of ways. Because the all-prevailing creative power of God encompasses us, the power of love is at our command.

We activate the power of Oneness by applying the organizing principle of Oneness in our words and deeds as we perform our role as secondary agents of creation on our subjective and individual plane. As our children witness us applying the Oneness principle, they learn the power of Oneness. This is our purpose in being here; Oneness is our job. Only this is consistent with being created in the likeness and image of a loving God.

The second fundamental human nature taught by religion is our failure to live in a way that is consistent with our God-given nature because we are inherently flawed—born into sin, some would say. This is offered as an explanation of why we cause all manner of misery when acting contrary to our God-given nature—when we are applying the disorganizing process of duality— and it helps complete the story of good versus evil. Evil, we are told, reflects the flawed part of our nature. It dooms us to misery, but many religions claim to have the keys—the right ritual, the right sacrifice or belief—to unlock Heaven, promising escape from the doom that awaits all the others.

The story of how human failure of this magnitude originally came about varies from one religious tradition to another, but many religions acknowledge a separation or fall from grace exists and that there is a duty to address it. Doing so has been slow in coming.

The divide between our God-like nature and our fallen nature is the basis for asserting that some people are inherently good (us and our allies) and others are inherently evil (our enemies). After all, we are the chosen few. This belief, in turn, leads to the related belief that we are unconnected to those who are evil, and that their wrongful acts are done independent of our own acts, words, or deeds. Modeling a vengeful God, we are to impose punishment and retribution on those who violate our norms. Messages such as "spare the rod and spoil the child" tell us any other approach is a weak or ineffective response to disobedience or conflict.

In the end, the conflicting images of humankind can only be resolved by understanding that they reflect two mind-sets, the underlying structures of Oneness and duality. When we apply Oneness, we see goodness inherent in all of life, despite the storms about us. When we apply duality, we live in isolation, chasms between us, what we fear, and those whom we label evil. When we apply the disorganizing process of duality and call it good, we are confused.

Our God-given free will enables us to choose to act in concert with either the organizing principle of Oneness or duality. Neither negates our having been created in the likeness and image of God. Seeing God as omnipotent, omnipresent, and omniscient, without exception, means God encompasses our manifest or physical/mental nature, even that which we call evil and the state of sin.

Our two natures do not prove duality is real or that evil exists. Regardless of how evil we deem a person to be, no one can exist outside of the principle of Oneness without destroying Oneness's all-inclusive nature—and this neither we nor they possess the power to accomplish. Our relationship to Oneness is governed by universal principles that are equally applicable to everyone, whether they belong to one religion or to another or to none at all.

In understanding the principle of Oneness, religious teachings about the omnipotence of God, and that God is love, become comprehensible. It also means that God's love, unfailing guidance, provision, and protection are available to everyone without regard to race, gender, ethnicity, nationality, IQ, formal education, or material wealth. Within it stand the homeless, the incarcerated, the churched and un-churched, the mentally ill, the rich, and the poor. No fee, sacrifice, or ritual is required for admission.

Rediscovering the Garden of Eden

Some religious teachings may start out as lessons in Oneness but, over time, they become distorted, reinterpreted to be a lesson that justifies duality. The ancient story of Adam and Eve is one example. A common version of the story explains that humankind is doomed to live in misery because Adam and Eve disobeyed the command of God by eating forbidden fruit. As an aside, because Eve enticed Adam, we are told that women are primarily to blame, and by extension the cause of at least some, if not all, of men's sins. This interpretation requires that critical details be ignored, but perhaps their importance makes sense only from the perspective of Oneness.

When we return to the story's origins, we find that *Eve* is an ancient word for "breath" or "the living soul." Adam calls her Eve because she is the mother of all living things, just as our thoughts are the cause of all that we manifest. *Adam* means "earth" or "physical being." Thus, we begin with the soul and the body of each of us, without exception.

Adam and Eve were the first couple—body and soul joined on Earth. They lived in paradise until Eve disobeyed God and brought home the forbidden fruit, which they ate. As the story goes, God punished them by expelling them from paradise to live in perpetual pain.

Contrary to popular belief, it is not an apple tree that was off limits. Adam and Eve were told that all the fruit in the garden was for their use, except the fruit of the tree of the *knowledge of good and evil,* "for in the day that thou eatest thereof thou shalt surely die."[39] Thus, we have the soul of humankind consuming a belief that divides us and can only lead to the body's misery and death.

A serpent tells Eve that the fruit of the forbidden tree will make them as gods; in other words, knowing good and evil. What Eve did not understand was that to think both good *and* evil are true is to be deceived, to enter into separation or duality. Adam and Eve's story, one that is as old as humankind, actually warns about the danger of dividing the world into good versus evil, us versus them, man against woman, nation against nation. Such beliefs contradict Oneness.

Only in duality is good pitted against evil, but to believe in both good and evil is the fall from grace, a stark denial that we are all equally made in the image and likeness of God. The belief in evil replaces the truth with the illusion of separation, the resulting fear leads to attacks, and peace is made impossible. As long as we think separation serves us, that our salvation—however that is defined—depends on being among the chosen few, we cannot let the illusion go. We thus evict ourselves from the Garden of Eden and place Oneness beyond our reach.

The story of Adam and Eve's fall from grace helps explain how we lose our way, why Oneness has been difficult to achieve, and why duality has been so tenacious. Recognizing the differences between Oneness and duality and how they operate in our world opens us to the possibility of the body and the living soul, symbolically called Adam and Eve, returning to the Garden of Eden by leaving duality behind.

Before God took Adam's rib to create Eve, "the Lord God caused a deep sleep to fall upon Adam,"[40] but no reference was ever made to him waking up. The time is at hand for Adam and Eve to awaken.

Religion and Oneness on Earth

While the concept of Oneness may be especially perplexing to Western minds, ingrained as they are in opposites like good versus evil and us versus them and the separation that such opposites imply, Jesus promised us Oneness on Earth. The often recited phrase in the Lord's Prayer. "Thy kingdom come, Thy will be done, on Earth as it is in Heaven," speaks of what is to be in this world. How could this be? Because Jesus was teaching us how to step out of duality and into the consciousness of Oneness.

Jesus was not the first to deliver a teaching like this. Five hundred years before Christ, Buddha taught that freedom from worldly illusions may be achieved by anyone who is disciplined and pursues the right *dhárma*[41] or virtuous path, thus enlightenment is accessible in this life. In the same time frame (fourth and third centuries BCE), the teachings of Taoism recognized the Great Way, the Tao, as a path to achieving spiritual grounding in this life.

The role of religion in making Earth as it is in Heaven is not to be underestimated. The institution of religion is uniquely suited to teach us how to achieve Oneness. By returning to its deepest roots, religion can relinquish its misguided subservience to duality, wherever it still exists, and champion the organizing principle of Oneness—at last.

Eight

SCIENCE AND REALITY

Quantum physics suggests that beyond the physical phenomena of the universe exists an infinite unified source of existence, a vast wholeness that contains all that is on every level.

Science is another critical thread, alongside religion, in the fabric of our understanding of Oneness and duality. A major scientific revolution began at the dawn of the twentieth century. The new science of quantum physics is rapidly deconstructing the old reality of separation and fragmentation, two characteristics essential to sustaining duality and justifying punitive justice. While it may remain largely unseen, as more people are formally educated and self-taught in the new science, the disorganizing process of duality is progressively losing legitimacy while the organizing principle of Oneness is taking its place as the new reality.

When I was young, reality was understood to be the mechanistic worldview of Newtonian physics and atomic theory. Both seemed to affirm the reality of a world made of separate material parts, and thus reinforced long-standing beliefs about duality. As a result of new discoveries, students are now being taught that we exist in a unified field of energy in which each part is a reflection of the whole so that when any part loses, the whole is diminished. This holographic theory of the universe is showing us that separation is an illusion—there is no divide between "us" and "them."

The shift from seeing only isolated parts of the whole to seeing that each part is integral to the whole is giving rise to a new conception of reality.

This new way of seeing reality is giving birth, for example, to exciting discoveries in the growing field of alternative and complementary medicine. In biology, it has led to the recognition that the wellness of the whole body is contingent upon the health of its individual cells. With science supporting interconnectedness as the "real" reality, we see that this interdependence applies to all systems—family, community, business, economics, education, religion, and culture. It means that the well-being of every institution depends on the well-being of every individual it touches and every function it serves.

How science defines reality has a major impact on the structure of the institutions within a system—law and government are no exception. This was demonstrated during the last scientific revolution, when Newtonian science indicated that the then existing governmental order was built on faulty beliefs. As a result, the governing hierarchy at the time—the church, and the monarchs, who had tied their legitimacy to these beliefs—were doomed to crumble as ruling institutions. The parallels between the Newtonian revolution and the changes in scientific thinking that we are now experiencing give reason to believe that monumental change is, once again, inevitable.

Comparisons

In the early 1600s, the first English settlers made their way to the North American continent, beginning with the landing of colonists in Jamestown in 1607 and the Pilgrims' founding of Plymouth in 1620. Jamestown and Plymouth marked the commencement of a steady stream of European immigrants settling in the New World, where they were no longer forced to live within the strict confines of the old order. (The Internet is providing us with a liberation of similar magnitude, as discussed in chapter 14.)

Just as these settlers were getting established, Galileo (1564–1642), like Copernicus before him, asserted that Earth revolves around the Sun. At the time, established church doctrine taught that God had placed Earth first in the universal realm. This justified the claim of the church and monarch that they had a God-given right to govern because they held the exalted station in the earthly realm. The people's submission to the divine right of kings and church authority was tethered to the old cosmic order. By refuting the centrality of Earth, the scientific findings in Galileo's work threatened the authority and control of the institutions of government. The new science meant that the demise of the divine right of kings was inevitable.

The erosion of church domination continued as the scientific discoveries of Isaac Newton (1642–1727) and others continued to redefine reality. In the end, Newtonian science ended the preoccupation of governing institutions with God's realm and replaced it with a focus on the physical laws of matter. In fact, in Newton's universe, God is unnecessary.

As the assault on church hierarchy and its theology widened, science and religion became rivals; monarchs declined, and new forms of government were envisioned in which the people would be supreme. The old order was in collapse. Newtonian science was shaping a new reality, and in so doing charting the course of modern history.

Many were excited by the thought that a mathematically based, scientific knowledge of the material world was possible in lieu of the inconsistencies of religious systems. The religious wars that began in 1562 and did not end until the Peace of Westphalia in 1648 were still a relatively fresh memory. For nearly a hundred years, Christians had slaughtered Christians over which form of religion was right, Catholicism or Protestantism. In the end, science terminated the ancient connection between religion and political control, something many saw as a cause for celebration. They had yet to discover the fallacies of Newtonian science.

Fundamental to Newtonian science was atomic theory, first proposed by Democritus more than two thousand years ago. This theory held that the world was constituted of separate atoms made up of a nucleus, neutrons, and protons, moving about in the void of empty space. Thus, the classical physics of Newton is also called material, physical, or scientific realism, implying that this formulation of science and material realism are inseparable. Newtonian science appeared to be supported by scientific experiments that generally confirmed the fragmented atomic view and materialism.

Over time, this material-centric worldview led most people in the Western world to believe that the ever-changing forms and characteristics of all objects were the result of different arrangements of the bits of matter in moving atoms. Even human beings came to be understood in terms of structures and functions of aggregates of separate atoms. Nature and man became separate. Traditions that honored nature with a spirit equal to man's were dismissed as animistic, primitive, and pagan. This separatist view of reality meant that what happened in one place had no relation to what happened in another; what one person thought or believed was unrelated to the whole. In this construct, there was no meaningful way to deal with consciousness, mind, or soul.

The new materialism found moral legitimacy by interpreting the Judeo-Christian story of creation in the Old Testament as confirmation of man's superiority over nature. The passage that says God gave man "dominion over the fish of the sea, and over the fowl of the air, and over the cattle, and over all the earth, and over every creeping thing that creepeth upon the earth"[42] was taken to mean humankind could do with nature whatever served its needs and wants. This view of reality allowed scientists and political leaders to treat the material world like a huge lifeless machine, waiting for man's manipulation and control.

Beginning with the seventeenth century, the atomistic, fragmented way of seeing the world came to permeate nearly every aspect of our culture—law, government, economics, social order—as well as science. Just as outward appearances had informed those living in an earlier era that the Earth was the center of the universe, outward appearances led us to believe that we are physical beings, separate from other physical beings. This immersion in fragmentation reinforced the belief that separation (duality) reflected the real world. Evidence to the contrary was overlooked or discounted.

The manner in which mind was deemed separate from matter made it difficult to recognize that the principles of material realism are philosophical in nature, mere assumptions about the nature of being that are not supported by experiment or scientific measurement. With the advent of quantum physics, the scientific evidence indicated otherwise. Physicist David Bohm explains that scientists later realized the notion of atomism led to confused questions and that the experimental confirmation of the atomic point of view was limited,[43] an error unrecognized until the twentieth century.

The roots of fragmentation are now so deep and pervasive that we continuously try to divide and isolate elements of a larger system that is, in fact, one and indivisible.[44] In so doing, the monarch and religion have been replaced with new hierarchies, reshaping who is authorized to control, impose judgment, and punish.

The Modern Era

Despite its flaws, the focus of Newtonian physics on the laws of matter led to amazing success in sustaining material progress. It ushered in the modern era and led to the rapid industrial and technological development of Europe and the United States during the nineteenth century. In turn, the demands of the Industrial Revolution put pressure on the decentralized delivery of governmental services, forcing government organizations to change—all in the name of material reality. Our governmental system went from a loosely connected grid of small central governments with limited authority to an ever-growing centralized bureaucracy.

Industrialization required a model of government that could meet the needs for mass transportation systems, roads and bridges, universal education, and massive water and sewer systems.[45] Educational institutions were designed on the industrial model with children learning to be productive assembly-line workers in school buildings that often looked like factories. Corporations were invented, a means of organizing and managing material assets in perpetuity and maximizing shareholder profit. The corporate structure, however, broke the link between ownership and accountability to the community.

As industry and technology grew, government came to serve the needs of huge corporate conglomerates, such as those in agriculture, energy, pharmaceuticals, media, the military-industrial complex, and the prison-industrial complex. Many came to see the purpose of government and education as serving the needs and interests of these structures, and not, as the founding fathers had envisioned, as serving the needs and interests of all people. Democracy fell short of its hoped-for transformation as the industrial hierarchy replaced the monarch, still leaving the interests of the people marginalized.

How did this materialistic world deal with conflict? By developing methods and machines to defeat and control those who threatened the interests of the new ruling order. Newtonian materialism and technology-driven war fit together like a hand in a glove and led to military industrialization.

The twentieth century, the pinnacle of the modern era, opened with World War I, in which nearly twenty million died. It was not long before World War II consumed much of the world, a war in which an estimated fifty to sixty million died. During all of the twentieth century, Communist oppression alone may account for more than sixty million deaths. Include the Korean War, the Vietnam War, and multitudes of separate atrocities, and the twentieth century adds up to the bloodiest in history. The decision makers who ordered these deaths nearly always saw them as justified—deeds they were forced to commit by their proclaimed evil enemies.

Leaders ruling from within this dualistic mentality, who are in control of modern weapons capable of wiping out humanity, do not bode well for our survival. Their mind-set quickly reduces life to a question of survival at any cost, blinding them to the whole. It is collective insanity, causing the leadership of diverse nations to be held in the iron grip of old, reactive patterns. Seeing the world as fragmented and ourselves as separate has not served us well. We must open to new insights that are as different from atomic theory as atomic theory was from the theories that preceded it.[46] The new scientific revolution is answering this need.

Quantum Physics

The twentieth century opened not only with bloodshed and war, but also with the birth of another revolution in science: quantum physics. While it is an oversimplification, atomic theory came into question with the discovery that light could manifest both as waves and particles, an idea that was inconceivable in the old science that saw matter (i.e., the particle) as primary. It was a contradiction of the old order's logic that went to its core, indicating something was fundamentally wrong with established theory.

Atomic theory assumes that distant objects cannot directly influence each other, since it appears an object can be influenced only by a force within its immediate surroundings. As quantum physics developed, this proved to be another unworkable theory. The new physics indicates that distant systems are not independent. It has been observed that when a particle is split and the two parts locate to different places in the universe, a change in the spin on one part results in an instantaneous change in the spin of the second part in an identical way, without time lapsing for information to travel from one part to the other. They operate within a greater whole that we do not yet understand.

Further discovery determined that the quantum realm is holographic, meaning that each part, while appearing to be a separate event, is a microcosm of the whole—everything is inextricably linked. Thus, quantum physics is disproving the theory that we live in separation, unconnected to others and unaffected by what happens to them. Instead, as you do to others, you literally do to yourself. There is no division between the observer and the observed because the act of observing changes both the observer and the observed, making objective reality impossible to observe. Bohm explains, "Rather, both observer and observed are merging and interpenetrating aspects of one whole reality, which is indivisible and unanalysable."[47] Instead of an atomistic us-and-them view of the world, we are now moving toward the realization that only Oneness can be real.

Atomic theory not only saw mind and matter as separate, it assumed that matter preceded consciousness—that consciousness in some way bubbled up out of primordial mud. The theory now is that consciousness precedes matter; it most likely creates the mud. We create the world we experience through the underlying mental structure that we activate—Oneness or duality. Transmitting the impulse of love activates the principle of Oneness and creates a life characterized by harmony and balance, while transmitting the impulse of fear activates duality and brings forth chaos and pain.

A growing number of scientists share this view. Physicist Fred Alan Wolf writes:

[I]f you have fearful images, they tend to come into reality; whatever you can imagine begins to appear as if we called it into existence. . . . [The universe] says whatever you create as imagery, so will it be. Why? Because at the core of the universe, at its most fundamental level, it is not solid stuff. It is not hard reality. It is capable of forming reality into whatever our images produce.

All political and social systems are produced this way. They are all magnifications of this basic misunderstanding of the nature of this hidden aspect of reality. If people could comprehend the imaginal element in all matter, then what they envision would eventually come to pass. . . . [I]t may or may not come to pass at this instant, but it begins to manifest at the level of dreams.[48]

Quantum physics suggests that beyond the physical phenomena of the universe exists an infinite unified source of existence, a vast wholeness that contains all that is on every level. We can purposefully engage this realm in a mutually beneficial union. This presents the possibility that the next stage in human evolution may not be in the physical body, as in the past, but in the depths of human consciousness, as we learn to intentionally activate the principle of Oneness.

The Seeds of Reconciliation
Between Science and Religion

As discussed in chapter 7, the concept of Oneness has been a prevalent concept in religion from the beginning. Perhaps one of the most surprising developments to come from the new science is this: lessons of the spiritual masters about the Oneness of life are being affirmed by new scientific discoveries. The new science is supportive of religion's return to its roots in Oneness—another example of interconnectedness. In this respect, the new scientific matrix is in alignment with the ancient realm; both affirm that to love one's neighbor as oneself is good for all of us, because we are each part of an all-encompassing whole.

Religion and science now have a bridge to a shared reality. As both help inform our understanding of Oneness, for the first time since Descartes philosophized about the primacy of matter, the institutions of religion, science, and the humanities can work together to design structures, such as unitive justice, that support Oneness instead of duality. As more people come to share the belief that Oneness is the true nature of reality, there will arise a growing demand for institutional change that creates peace and harmony.

Change Is Inevitable

Though it has proven to be a flawed system, even one plagued with disaster, the old order built on material reality has been in existence for a long time. In the face of such intransigence, is it reasonable to consider the possibility of a change as monumental as Oneness replacing duality? Can new institutions, such as unitive justice, become the norm?

Not only can this occur, it must. With the science of quantum physics redefining our reality as a unified field, punitive justice and other dualistic structures no longer make sense. Why would we intentionally harm others, as punitive justice requires, once we realize that at the same time we also harm ourselves? As discussed earlier in the chapter, we have had a monumental shift of this magnitude in the past, and conditions are ripe for it to happen once again. One question remains. Will the old order of duality, with its ready access to modern weapons of mass destruction, lead to self-annihilation before the new order takes hold?

The worldview of duality can lead to extinction. However, the material discussed in chapters 14 and 15 provides evidence that the emergence of growing numbers of institutions built on the principle of Oneness is already creating a new and higher order of humanity.

Nine

ONENESS AND THE NATION-STATE

There are politicians who do not consciously realize
they are part of a larger, destructive pattern,
because they don't look at the big picture.

The organizing principles of Oneness and duality not only apply on the individual level and the community level, but they apply at the level of the nation-state as well. When duality is the path chosen at the national level, the scope of the harm done is magnified. As there are nations that now possess technology with the capacity to extinguish all life, we can easily calculate the risk of remaining chained to duality.

On the other hand, when Oneness is the chosen path, the good done by the nation-state is large scale. Compelling evidence of the destructive nature of dualistic state action and the positive effect of state action guided by Oneness is found in a series of events that occurred during the war in Iraq.

In the wake of the Iraq War, Muslims in many countries turned against the United States, wishing Americans harm and even death. In Pakistan, favorable public opinion toward the United States plummeted to just a few percentage points. Then Pakistan was hit with a terrible earthquake in October 2005. American soldiers were sent to Pakistan to give earthquake victims medical care, shelter, and food. By doing so, they won the hearts of many Pakistanis who had previously hated Americans. Favorable opinion toward the United States rose to 46 percent by the end of November of that year.[49]

Then in January 2006, Americans returned to the method of an eye for an eye in Pakistan. Gunfire from CIA drones missed the intended target, instead killing eighteen innocent men, women, and children in a remote village. Pakistanis were outraged. Crowds took to the streets chanting threats to the Americans. By August 2007, only 19 percent reported a favorable opinion of the United States; a mere 9 percent were favorable toward President George W. Bush. It was Osama bin Laden whose favorable approval rating then stood at 46 percent.[50]

What happened? The actors were the same: the United States and Pakistan. The Iraq War was still in full force when the radical shift in Pakistani opinion toward the United States occurred. The answer is clear. The earthquake relief effort was the Golden Rule at work—the human needs of people being addressed, not a political agenda aimed at getting them to do or think as we want. While it had been thought that it would take years for nearly half of all Pakistanis to again hold a favorable public opinion toward the United States, it had been achieved in a month of action grounded in Oneness. With our return to the punitive approach, it was quickly undone. This pattern is no longer shrouded in mystery.

Good and Evil in the Eye of the Beholder

After graduating from college, I joined the Peace Corps and served for two years in Nepal from 1965 to 1967, during the height of the Vietnam War. I left for Nepal at a time when many young men my age were being drafted. Among the Peace Corps volunteers I served with, there were frequent discussions about the war and little agreement on whether the men, upon completion of their service in Nepal, should then serve in the military. I believed they shouldn't question their duty to serve our nation. We were, I reasoned, the good fighting the evil.

On the trip home from Nepal, I visited Saigon to see that war-torn area for myself. A young helicopter pilot I met at the USO described how the rivers ran red with blood when he flew into a battle zone to deliver troops or pick up the wounded—the blood of both sides.

Robert McNamara was secretary of defense during the Vietnam War. When I heard him speak around 2005, he confessed to how little he had understood the enemy. Years after the war, he met with some of the leaders of the Vietcong forces. They told McNamara that, after years of subservience to the French, the Vietnamese were determined to be free of Western domination—at any cost. At the same time, their distrust of the Chinese spanned centuries. From their perspective, an alliance with the Chinese was thrust upon them to defend against American force, not because they wanted to become a puppet of the Chinese regime or, as Americans were told at the time, be part of a Communist conspiracy to rule the world.

With the passage of time, McNamara expressed regret about having learned so little about the hopes, dreams, and fears of the Vietnamese before assuming they were our enemies. "We must try to put ourselves inside [our enemies'] skin and look at us through their eyes," he later admonished.[51] Many mistakes ensued from his fragmented, dualistic view of the people of Vietnam, and thousands, even millions, of lives were needlessly lost.

As he struggled to make sense of his part in the Vietnam War, McNamara struggled as well with an earlier moral dilemma. During World War II he had performed statistical analysis for General Curtis E. LeMay and the Army's Air Forces. America's firebombing of Japanese cities during the war killed perhaps as many as nine hundred thousand Japanese civilians. McNamara recalled LeMay saying, "If we'd lost the war, we'd all have been prosecuted as war criminals."

A question McNamara could never answer was, "What makes it immoral if you lose and not immoral if you win?"[52] In later years, McNamara concluded LeMay was right—in so far as the killing of so many Japanese civilians was involved, the Americans had behaved as war criminals. Despite his being accustomed to dual morality, he could not project enough blame upon the Japanese to make the United States blameless in the deaths of so many noncombatants.

Attack Is a Double-Edged Sword

History records that the Allies won World War II. To win, our government had funded private scientific exploration to achieve advances in technology that seemed miraculous, including the development of nuclear bombs capable of instantly torching masses of people. Most who engaged in developing these weapons were motivated by a deep desire to achieve peace, and saw bigger and better weapons as the means. In terms of conventional thinking, the United States had played a major role in achieving victory in World War II without any harm to the then forty-eight states. As our lens expands, we see the outcome is not so clear-cut.

When you attack another, you attack yourself. The CIA calls it blowback. Nuclear weapons now present a constant threat to the security of Americans. With time, U.S. technological innovation also led to the invention of small, destructive, and easily accessible weapons. These weapons now enable guerrilla armies and those whom we call terrorists to engage our military in attacks and counterattacks. The weapons Americans invented to promote peace—both large and small—are now used to threaten the lives of Americans, as well as many people of diverse nations.

As he left office in 1960, President Dwight Eisenhower warned the American people about the growing military-industrial complex.

The means used to end a terrible war, namely pro-militarism, was becoming a lasting legacy. The use of overwhelming force as the way we address challenges has become an American mind-set. Not including its nuclear weapons, the wars, veterans, and homeland security, the U.S. defense budget now constitutes about half of what the world spends on defense.[53]

By the beginning of the twenty-first century, the United States had amassed a nuclear arsenal that included 5,400 multiple-megaton warheads based on land and sea, 1,750 nuclear bombs and cruise missiles ready to be delivered by air, 1,670 so-called tactical nuclear weapons, and 10,000 nuclear warheads laying in wait in bunkers around the country.[54] To what end? Only in duality's snare could this occur. More is better is not a tenet that can rationally be applied to weapons designed to instantly annihilate masses of humanity.

More than our material abundance or our invasive pop culture, "the nation's arsenal of high-tech weaponry and the soldiers who employ that arsenal have come to signify who and what we stand for.[55] "[A] vast network of American military bases on every continent except Antarctica actually constitutes a new form of empire."[56]

Whenever it serves our interests, as they are defined at the time, this us-versus-them worldview tells us we can always win by having the capacity to force others to physically lose. Our policies are largely driven by a need to defeat external enemies rather than to solve internal challenges. We could have chosen, instead, to provide better services to our people, to tax them less, or share more of our abundance with others. The path we chose leaves the threads of community sorely frayed, and peace difficult to achieve.

The Seduction of Dualistic Self-Interest

The state of the criminal law system described in chapter 1 is shocking. One is compelled to ask, how is it that a nation like the United States, known for its commitment to liberty and justice for all, became embedded in an incarceration binge of such magnitude? Examining this evolution provides important lessons about how the disorganizing process of duality feeds on self-interest.

Duality uses fear to provoke action. For nearly forty years, to get themselves elected, U.S. politicians have used the get-tough punitive approach to crime to convert complex problems into simple slogans that play on our fear of crime. They didn't tell us that their get-tough-on-crime policies had little effect on the rate of violent crime, even though by the 1990s the evidence was clear. They were primarily locking up nonviolent offenders. Between 1980 and 1993, nonviolent offenders accounted for 84 percent of the growth in state and federal prison populations.[57] Nonetheless, once elected, the politicians continued to pass laws and adopted policies that take the punitive form of justice to greater and greater extremes. Why?

From 1950 to 1960, the number of televisions in U.S. homes grew from nineteen million to forty-seven million. As television took over as our main entertainment and source of information, the media, politicians, and pollsters became more savvy about how to use feelings, images, and thirty-second sound bites to shape how Americans vote. They discovered that our fear of crime is easily manipulated and can be used to mobilize voters, even if it means the collateral damage must be kept under wraps and it does little to change the crime rate.

The late 1960s and early 1970s were the turning point. In 1970, there were only 196,429 men and women in state and federal prisons.[58] Just two years before, the assassination of Martin Luther King Jr. had sparked race riots across the country.

The 1968 presidential campaign between Richard Nixon and Hubert Humphrey was the first to market the presidential candidates as if they were consumer products.[59] What better ribbon to tie that package together than our fear of crime? This is what Nixon said in one of his takes for a television campaign ad:

> I say that when crime has been going up nine times as fast as population, when we've had riots in three hundred cities that have cost us two hundred dead and seven thousand injured, when forty-three percent of the American people are afraid to walk in the streets of their cities at night, then it's time for a complete housecleaning, it's time for a new attorney general, it's time to wage an all-out war on crime in the United States. I pledge that kind of activity. And I pledge to you that we will again have freedom from fear in the cities and in the streets of America.[60]

It was a time of turbulence for the nation, and we were offered more vengeance as the answer. Within a decade, the incarceration rate nationwide began to surge upward at an unprecedented rate.[61]

In the 1980s, politicians began to see thirty-second sound bites about crime as essential campaign tools. They crafted snappy messages, like "the war on drugs," "abolish parole," "truth in sentencing," "three strikes, you're out," "mandatory minimums," "zero tolerance," and "try juveniles as adults." These clever sound bites were translated into more punitive laws that have deeply impacted the system, all in accordance with the rule of law. Getting tough on crime has become a crusade, used even when crime rates are falling. There are politicians who do not consciously realize they are part of a larger, destructive pattern, because they don't look at the big picture.

The politicians were not alone in using fear of crime to serve their self-interests. Sensationalizing crime by the media draws and

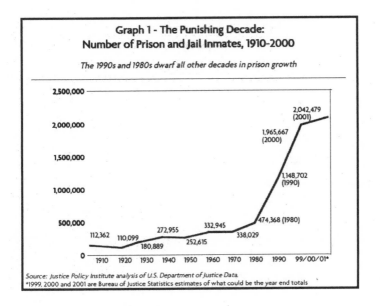

**Graph 1 - The Punishing Decade:
Number of Prison and Jail Inmates, 1910-2000**

The 1990s and 1980s dwarf all other decades in prison growth

Source: Justice Policy Institute analysis of U.S. Department of Justice Data.
*1999, 2000 and 2001 are Bureau of Justice Statistics estimates of what could be the year end totals

retains viewers. Simply put, it increases the viewing audience, and that sells ad time. We now so often see crime scenes, hear crime reports, and listen to victims of crime that we easily conclude there is nowhere we are safe.

The United States has experienced sustained falling crime rates since 1991, achieving levels last witnessed in the 1960s. Nonetheless, the rate of incarceration has increased dramatically during that time. While some argue that the reduction in crime is due to the fact so many of our citizens are behind bars, one examination of the rise of imprisonment from 1992 to 2001 led to the conclusion that the *entire* increase in incarceration was a result of stiffer sentencing policy and practice.[62]

It is now standard political practice to label candidates who object to this wasteful path and propose better answers as being soft on crime, which, in an environment of vengeance at any cost, makes them a target. While tough on crime is an easy sell, the assertion that this excessively punitive approach is good public policy is refuted, not only by the Pew Report mentioned in chapter 1, but by a stream of earlier reports, studies, books, and documentaries that have been warning us of an impending crisis for a long time.

Dr. Karl Menninger wrote *The Crime of Punishment* in 1966, even before the U.S. incarceration binge began. He tells us about two disturbed young men who had pointlessly killed a younger friend. In a compromise, life sentences were imposed instead of death. While incarcerated, one was killed by a fellow prisoner. After the other spent many years in prison, a number of people helped him secure parole. He worked in a hospital laboratory until he was fifty; then he went to college. After graduation, he served for four years as research associate and project director in the Department of Health. Menninger asks, as a society, was this the right decision, or "should we have held to the ancient, savage ritual of confinement and punishment, and continued his slow suffocation at public expense?"[63]

So far, our society has favored the ancient, savage ritual of punitive justice for which we all pay a price. We are offered forced compliance, at the expense of meaningful, transformative change. We have acquiesced as the politicians continue to write the laws that sustain this failed policy, blind to its excessive costs.

Once begun, prison expansion developed its own political momentum and economic drivers, despite its lack of social benefit or value-added product. It now has a life all its own, making politicians and the prison-industrial complex the benefactors. We are left with a severely broken correctional system, not to mention the broken lives, broken families, and broken communities it reaps. While the United States is unique in many respects and it does provide a large degree of freedom for most of its citizens, when duality takes hold on a national scale, the results are always tragic.

Choosing Oneness over Duality

I spent my sophomore year of college in Paris, France, just nine-teen years after the end of World War II. The college program fo-cused on the newly established European Economic Community, as the European Union (EU) was called in those early days. They were building a unified community among former enemies who, for centuries, had been divided by culture, language, and war. As a young adult, I recognized the importance of this endeavor, but I was not aware how rarely nations choose this path.

In Paris I lived in the home of a French widow who vividly recalled Germany's occupation of France. The Germans were de-spised. Though it was not popular, President Charles DeGaulle reminded the French of the two world wars Europe had recently experienced. If war was to be avoided in the future, he said, their hatred had to be set aside to forge a union based on shared eco-nomic interests. The EU now extends beyond dropping trade barriers to include legislation, security, an evolving united legal system, and a unified currency. This is an example of how, once we let go of the us-versus-them mentality, we see that, in the end, what we held on to so tightly had little value.

During my year abroad, we spent Easter week in West Berlin. On Easter Sunday, 1963, we went through Checkpoint Charlie, through the newly constructed Berlin wall, and spent the day in East Berlin. I saw a people living in terror, not of invaders, but of their own repressive government, a puppet of the Soviet Union. The power of the people can be abused when those in control of government are able to maintain control through fear. When the Berlin wall fell in 1989, it affirmed that no government can re-press a people who unite in their innate need to be free and loving. In Oneness there is power.

During the brief six-month window before the Berlin wall was dismantled, I returned to the wall with my sixteen-year-old son and my younger daughter who was fourteen. It was Easter, 1990. This time I watched as my two children stood on that wall, with no fear, chipping off souvenirs with hammers and chisels rented from a nearby huckster.

In the spring of 2005, I was in Paris on a study trip. It was just weeks before several countries of Eastern Europe, countries previously locked within the walls of communism, were to become members of the European Union. In my lifetime, DeGaulle's vision of a united Europe was coming to maturity.

In 1963, I saw the forced control that the Berlin wall imposed on the fearful people of East Berlin. In 1990, I saw the Berlin wall for what it truly was—mortar and sand, a wall that had no power other than the power the people it was meant to entomb had surrendered to it. In 2005, I saw that, when we set aside our fears and join together, we possess a power no individual can achieve, and tyrants have no ability to extinguish.

The Just War Doctrine

When the state needs to justify its dualistic choices, it sometimes seeks support from religious teachings. We see this crossover in the Just War Doctrine, a credo shared by many Christian denominations that has been used to give the churches' blessings to a number of wars, past and present.

The need for a church doctrine that addressed war arose early on, when Roman Emperor Constantine the Great (circa 280–337 CE) became the first Christian emperor and made Christianity the official religion in the fourth century. This gave rise to philosophical differences that had to be dealt with. As the emperor, he used his armies as his means to sustain control of the Roman Empire. As a Christian ruler unwilling to give up his armies, he needed to reconcile the teachings of Christ with militarism.

Constantine named himself high priest of the institutionalized church and decided which church leaders and church doctrines would hold sway. This enabled the emperor to entwine the aims of the church with the aims of the empire, even before it became official church doctrine.

The inception of the Just War Doctrine as church law is traced to the theologian Augustine in the fifth century, although he drew upon established Roman practices[64] and the tradition of punitive justice that extended back to well before the time of Moses. While no doubt originally intended to limit war, or control the conditions of war, in so doing, it has had the significant effect of condoning war.

The doctrine holds that war is moral if it is executed in accordance with certain tests that Augustine defined as follows: right authority, a just cause, right intent, the prospect of success, proportionality of good to evil done, and that war is a last resort.[65] The problem with these tests is this: any aggressor, by his own measure, can claim to have met them all.

The test of right authority is easily met if the aggressor is a state. A just cause, from the aggressor's perspective, is a given. As for intent, no leader or general claims to go to war to achieve evil or unnecessary harm. The prospect of success is often pure speculation for which little objective evidence is likely to exist. Proportionality of good to evil done is a matter of perspective based upon what interests are at stake. That war is a last resort has been claimed even when the enemy is not planning an attack, as in the Iraq War. Each test being subjective, the Just War Doctrine provides a form, without substance, for justifying war.

The fact that the Just War Doctrine does not include the question, are you doing unto others as you would have them do unto you? is not an oversight—it is a test that war cannot pass. As a result, rather than providing a safe haven for the oppressed, the church has too often accommodated the state by permitting church doctrine to serve the aggressor.

Our Choices

For the foreseeable future, state and federal institutions will be charged with protecting the public from threats that are beyond the capacity of the community to remediate. But direct involvement of victims, offenders, and community members as key participants with decision-making authority is the best route to local peace and order. Local peace is the key, for a peaceful nation exists when each community within it experiences peace.

As we begin to understand how the mental structures of Oneness and duality manifest on the physical plane, there is no need for judgment or blame. It is because we were blinded by our belief in separation, unable to perceive ourselves as integral parts of the all-encompassing whole, that our public policies were not aligned with our highest good.

Our perception of separation has been a painful state of existence, but we now have the opportunity to choose differently, thought by thought, one action after another. By choosing to implement the organizing principle of Oneness and act from loving-kindness, we discover that self-interest means attending to the self in harmony with the whole. The founding fathers of the United States spoke of what is possible in a nation whose citizens choose Oneness when they wrote the Declaration of Independence:

> We hold these truths to be self-evident, that all men are created equal, that they are endowed by their Creator with certain unalienable Rights, that among these are Life, Liberty and the pursuit of Happiness.

Ten

THE LANGUAGE OF
ONENESS AND DUALITY

*If we are to set aside the old patterns, we must create
language that draws clear distinctions between the
underlying mental structures of Oneness and duality.*

We have fallen from grace, so to speak, by getting ourselves trapped
in duality, but the science of quantum physics is a major lever moving us toward Oneness. One obstacle is the fact that our language
is often so imprecise, even contradictory, that it promotes confusion between these two mental systems. Understanding the choice
we have between punitive justice and unitive justice, for example,
is made more difficult because we use the term *justice* to describe
both.

I won is another imprecise term. When I say, "I won," it is not
clear if this included or excluded others winning as well. It would
be more accurate to say that I defeated my opponent, if that is
what happened, instead of saying I won. When *winning* means the
imposition of control and retribution, as punitive justice seeks to
do, it ignores what has been lost. Unitive justice recognizes that no
one wins until everyone does, so the verb *to win* is best used only
in the context of a win-win outcome.

Language can be framed to influence what we think. Sometimes language virtually does the thinking for us by answering our

questions before they are asked. The distinctions can be subtle, or designed to deal with sensitive subjects. Human killing is a good example, a subject we rarely want to identify so clearly. When executions are carried out on behalf of the state, they are called the death penalty, telling us these deaths were deserved. When our soldiers kill innocent people, they are dismissed as collateral damage, telling us not to bother about those deaths, as they were necessary to achieve some other objective. When we kill our enemies, it is heroism rewarded with medals and stars that denote patriotism. When our own are killed, it is terrorism or murder, meaning these deaths are not to be tolerated. All of these reflect the disorganizing process of duality. Even when they fall within the letter of the law, they violate the principle of Oneness.

Without clear language, politicians can talk of peace when they mean war. A tiny part of a problem can be made the focus so that what's happening in the larger realm, such as corruption at the top or abuse throughout, is ignored.

If we are to set aside the old patterns, we must create language that draws clear distinctions between the underlying mental structure of Oneness and that of duality. We have already seen the issue of language arise several times in previous chapters as we have sought to distinguish these concepts. Here are some suggested terms for building a working vocabulary to better communicate about these two diverse realms, including some terms previously mentioned.

Discernment Versus Judgment

As we attempt to more clearly express our intended meaning, it is important to avoid seeing Oneness and duality as just another form of dualistic good versus evil. Distinguishing between judgment and discernment will help in this regard.

Judgment is nearly always the projection of a negative assessment upon another person or thing, along with the belief that it is real. We judge another to be guilty, lazy, ugly, or undesirable. While a positive opinion of another can be achieved by judging, it is relative and within a hierarchy that discounts others, like choosing Miss Universe. The unavoidable consequence of judgment is separation from that which we judge.

Judgment reflects our attachment to how we think things should be and our lack of peace with how they are. We resort to judgment, projecting good and evil as a distorted guide in choosing between the opposites we imagine exist. As judgment proliferates, separation from one another is magnified and human relations deteriorate.

An insidious use of judgment is to justify the use of force or abuse to impose control by those who are dominant. At the same time, they project blame for their actions on those whom they dominate by judging them as deserving of nothing better. We see this demonstrated in chapter 12 by the guards in the Stanford Prison Experiment when they blame their abusive conduct on the prisoners.

To discern, on the other hand, is to recognize differences and distinctions—to see clearly, without projection. Oneness consciousness is not a state in which everything is relative and anything goes. It is important to *discern* the path that will lead to our well-being and to peace, and to understand why. This requires discernment between what is real and what is illusion, a different process from judgment. Here is a concrete example of the difference.

Suppose someone who is dear to you is intelligent, fun to be with, generous, and a long list of other attributes. However, when you least expect it, an ancient wound opens up in this person and a victim emerges who sees a distorted meaning in some deed or words of yours that you never intended. This is a common scenario. When this happens, you have two choices. You can open your wounds and fire back with accusations of immaturity, jealousy, and even stupidity. This is judgment, and it leads to more conflict and pain.

Your other choice is to remain committed to the relationship and present to this moment of misunderstanding, not giving in to the temptation to counterattack. This enables you to assess what happened, identify what you did that triggered the fearful outbreak, explain your actual intent, and affirm that there was no intent on your part to slight, ignore, unfairly criticize, or hurt your friend. You focus on the positives and respond only to the core misunderstanding, doing so without judgment. This permits the conversation to continue until the storm has passed and you both are again in calm waters. You can also choose to welcome these episodes as opportunities for growth and transformation as discernment replaces judgment.

Being Innocent Versus Being Judged Innocent

Judgment brings up the issue of people who are found guilty or innocent by a judge in a court of law. In the legal system, to be judged innocent usually means there is insufficient evidence to be found guilty. This is the realm of duality.

On the level of Oneness, innocence means something quite different, for it is not an external attribute. It means to be pure, untainted, just as God created us. If we are created to exist in all-encompassing Oneness, then that remains our nature, despite any harmful or violent acts we may commit. As this type of innocence cannot be determined by outward appearances, or by projecting judgment upon another, if there is to be judgment in this realm, everyone must be judged only as innocent. Ultimately, we discover this is the only framing of innocence that is consistent and avoids the pitfalls of judgment.

We are not powerful enough to un-create the divine aspect of our core being. We do, however, have the free will to act in ways that may be contrary to it.

Power Versus Control

To have a meaningful discussion about Oneness and duality, we need specific action verbs that denote how people interact with others in each of these realms. Making a clear distinction between the terms *power* and *control* is an important first step.

We easily recognize the term *control* when used to mean the process of dominating others, restricting their freedom through physical, mental, or emotional coercion. Control is to wield influence using deception, magic, myth, or scare tactics, be they blatant or covert. Control is a territorial concept that is temporary, fleeting, and unpredictable. As rebellion is a constant threat, the person exercising control cannot sleep soundly for fear control will be lost when his back is turned. Slave masters, dictators, and occupiers know this all too well. Manipulating the physical level may achieve control, but it cannot achieve peace or transformation. Peace is a mental state that exists within us; it cannot be imposed from without.

To clarify our language, we can say that control is achieved through the use of attack, might, strength, force, coercion, violence, mechanisms, drive, or pressure. Those who impose control may attempt to disguise their intentions by using terms associated with Oneness, but control exists only in duality. Discord, disunity, and disharmony are the inevitable outcomes.

The term *power,* on the other hand, can be used to describe that quality possessed by those who draw others to join with them of their own free will. It is gained through integrity, honesty, respect, extending forgiveness, remorse, kindness, and generosity, by doing unto others as one would want done to oneself. The U.S. soldiers who extended aid to Pakistani earthquake victims in 2005, as described in chapter 9, were demonstrating American power and everyone benefited.

Power poses no physical, mental, or emotional threat. It has within it the strength of harmony, balance, and order. Power is constant, unwavering. The energy of power expands as it is shared. One with power knows peace, as did Buddha and Christ.

One with power can expose force for what it is—brutal and destructive. This is why those exercising power can use peaceful civil disobedience to defeat forceful attack. Mahatma Gandhi, barefooted and wearing a loincloth, led unarmed people and forced the British to surrender India by trumping control with power. How does this occur? A person dwelling in Oneness can overcome fear—our fear being something we each are able to master. Those who are free of fear are not subject to control, disarming those who need to impose control.

We think we must control when our belief in duality is strong, but control lacks legitimacy in the face of power. Investing in control costs us both our power and peace. Power, on the other hand, is inherently balanced and equitable and thus soundly legitimate. As we evolve toward Oneness, our power grows.

To Create Versus to Make

Other action verbs can be used in ways that clarify important distinctions. For example, in duality many things are of our own making. We make our chaotic world and we make enemies. It is helpful to use the verb *to make* to refer to action in this realm. Other useful verbs in describing action grounded in duality might be *to foster, to give rise to, to generate, to muster, to marshal, to manifest,* or *to cause.*

We can be more precise if we use the verb *to create* exclusively to refer to the domain of Oneness. We easily associate creating with a higher order. We create when we are being an individual expression of the Creator. We create peace, harmony, and loving relationships. Perhaps we need a new term, *co-make,* to refer to an alliance with someone else in the realm of duality, so we can reserve *co-creating* for joint action in Oneness.

Peace Versus Forced Compliance

Recently while listening to a show about the history of Japan, I heard the commentator note that there was an extended period of peace several centuries ago. Then the narrative went on to describe the brutality that had been used at the time to maintain what was called peace. However, it was not peace that was being experienced—it was forced compliance.

Punitive justice is dependent on forced compliance. Peace is the outcome of unitive justice. Peace is characterized by harmony, freedom, and abundance. It is not achieved through brutality or forced compliance.

Moral Values Versus Moral Judgment

Some people fall into the trap of confusing moral values with moral judgment. Moral values include the Golden Rule, kindness, honesty, integrity, and forgiveness—all attributes that characterize Oneness. People who exhibit these traits are moral.

Moral judgment is casting judgment based on differences in religious doctrines or other belief systems—a function of duality. For example, the term *family values* is a perfectly good term, but it is sometimes used as a code word for certain religious beliefs, and then those who do not ascribe to these beliefs are labeled immoral.

Declaring one side of a debate to be moral and the other side to be immoral based on differing political philosophies ignites anger and indignation. In this posture, each side works to get more people to join its so-called moral stance, fighting the immoral stance of the other side, and no one wins. We see this in elections when politicians, trying to build cohesion around separation, call the people who live in one place moral while asserting that the people who live in another place lack morality—small-town people versus urban dwellers, for example.

The I'm-right-you're-wrong stance of moral judgment leads some to feel justified in using the tools of government to impose their views on others. This leads to social conflict, the opposite of the social order they intend. Moral values, on the other hand, lead us to see others as deserving of our respect because they are human beings. Living in accordance with moral values creates lasting social order. Only moral values will lead us to peace.

Monomorality Versus Dual Morality

How is morality measured in the worldview of duality versus the worldview of Oneness? Duality's division between good and evil results in two standards of morality. Labeling themselves the good people, one side applies a standard of morality to themselves that they are unwilling to apply to those whom they see as evil. This enables the so-called good people to engage in destructive acts yet see their acts as moral and even to declare, "My killing is moral; yours is not." Their actions are rationalized by projecting responsibility and blame upon those to whom they are reacting.

"You hurt me! Since I'm good and you're bad, I can hurt you back, because you make me do it." This pattern of thinking permeates the school playground, the corporate boardroom, and the bloody battlefield. The practice of seeing oneself as not responsible for one's own intentional acts is an extreme form of victimization, a state of weakness. Yet it is this same thinking that justifies the inner workings of all punitive justice institutions.

To see others as evil is to fear them. Fear is a mental structure that relies on judgment. The first step is to correct the perception that underlies the judgment by extending love to those whom we fear—thus, we are commanded to love our enemies and to pray for those who persecute us.

As Oneness is consistent, one standard of morality is applied to all; there is no measuring our morality by the immorality of our enemies. We find this single standard in the universal principle of doing unto others as you would have them do unto you, a principle grounded in kindness. In Judaism and Christianity, this one moral standard is expressed in the Golden Rule. In other traditions it might be called lovingkindness, steadfast love, or, as in Islam, wishing for others what you wish for yourself. In the teachings of all major world religions, similar ethical principles call us to treat others with the kindness with which we want to be treated, providing us with a universal standard of morality, or *monomorality*.

Doing unto others as you would have them do unto you requires that you believe others deserve the same that you deserve, because you see them as equals. This requires an important distinction be made. Equality in this context is not a fear-based principle that applies to the physical and material world; it is a spiritual principle of the highest order. Every person is of equal value because that is their inherent nature—they were created equal, and they deserve to be loved, not for what they do or don't do, but because of who and what they are.

Love and kindness require that we treat others with dignity and respect, even when differences in beliefs, thoughts, or behaviors appear to separate them from us, and even when others do us harm. This does not happen haphazardly. When we consider what underpins kindness, we find it is the right use of will, or goodwill. It is the will to act in accord with Oneness, even as others try to inject the elements of duality, until individual action leads to harmony throughout the unified whole.

Forgiveness Versus Dispensation

We sometimes use the term *forgiveness* when we mean "dispensation." In one sense, we use the term *forgiveness* to refer to specific rites and rituals in which one of higher status, such as a priest, is authorized to give a dispensation to one of lower status, the penitent. This might better be called a ceremonial dispensation. We sometimes say that we will forgive another if he meets certain conditions, but we are prepared to withdraw our forgiveness if he fails along the way. This is more accurately called a conditional dispensation. Dispensation is of the world of duality.

The forgiveness that comports with Oneness, the forgiveness that heals, happens when the victim sees that there is nothing to forgive, to hold in account, or to trade for some reward of self-righteousness. All is just as it must be to facilitate transformation for victim and wrongdoer alike. It is an opportunity to restore love and to experience who we truly are—secondary agents of creation, manifesting lovingkindness in the physical realm, while asking nothing in return.

Forgiveness reflects the exercise of free will in shaping the outcome in favor of restoration and reconciliation, foregoing judgment and punishment, which only deepen the disharmony. Forgiveness has the power it does because it is not bound by linear cause and effect the way dispensation seems to be. We know forgiveness by its fruit: it touches the hearts and minds of those directly involved, but also extends beyond them, creating miracles along the way with no strings attached.

Egotranscendent Versus Egocentric

Ego is a term used in several different ways. If we define *ego* as "an inflated sense of one's own self-worth or superiority to others," we can build upon it to make another important distinction. *Egocentric* describes the state of being governed by one's ego and the fragmented, dualistic world that results. Preoccupation with one's own needs and interests blinds one to the interests of others. The disorganizing process of duality is at play when one is egocentric.

Egotranscendent describes the state of being beyond ego, not subject to its misperceptions, judgment, and sense of separation. In a state of egotranscendence, discernment of reality can occur. One's life becomes progressively egotranscendent as duality wanes because Oneness is embraced.

At this stage of our evolution, it is possible to intellectually comprehend what it means to be egotranscendent and yet be emotionally bound to the egocentric level, seemingly unable to escape. When this occurs, a person may even give lectures or write books about some aspect of Oneness, while treating family members, employees, or even adoring fans as though they are separate and inferior.

For many, this stage of simultaneously having a foot in the old world and the new may be unavoidable, a necessary rite of passage. One quickly learns that it does not result in harmony or happiness. Only when the principle of Oneness governs both the talk and the walk will the Garden of Eden's state of peace and abundance be accessible.

Freedom Versus Slavery

The terms *freedom* and *slavery* can provide a shorthand way to view how we interact with our environment. In duality's worldview, we believe we are slaves to our environment, having no control over what happens in our world. In this slave mentality, we are driven from one place to another with no understanding of the purpose being served. Why is this happening to me? is a question frequently asked when living in this condition. Enemies appear everywhere, attacking this way and that, forcing us to constantly plan our counterattacks as our freedom evaporates.

Consumed with fear, we place our faith in dogmas that condemn our enemies and affirm our innocence, even though such teachings are inconsistent. We grasp for one dogma or another that explains our fearful state and permits us to cling to our griev-ances. Each cherished grievance is an excuse to declare that if only something outside ourselves would change, we could be saved. This enslaved state persists because we cannot see that these cir-cumstances are the reflection of our own free will. Wedded to the illusion of separation, we become our own slave masters.

In the context of Oneness, freedom is defined as recognizing that we are the creators of the life we experience. We determine *what* we end up seeing by *how* we choose to see the world: through the inclusive reality of Oneness or the narrow projection of dual-ity. Oneness is already ours, for it is inherent within us; our task is simply to claim it as our own. Even a small doubt about the san-ity of duality is a step toward Oneness. As the momentum builds, someday we will be able to declare, "We are free at last," and it will be true.

Polarity Versus Duality

As suggested previously, the distinction between polarity and du-ality is essential for us to communicate effectively about the pro-cess of duality. To recap the characteristics of polarities, they are opposite properties that can be objectively tested and generally are not in dispute. Common examples include night and day, male and female, black and white, acid and alkaline. Polarities are an integral part of the physical world.

Duality has its own opposites, but they arise as a result of sub-jective perceptions and judgment. Duality's opposites are nearly always a matter of dispute, with little or no general agreement. These opposites depend on one's point of view or experience. Common examples are good and evil, pretty and ugly, delicious and unpalatable.

A common mistake is to think that good and evil are like night and day, but they are judgments; one person's judgment about who or what is evil may be widely disputed by others. Good versus evil is an example of duality, not polarity.

A word of caution is in order: If we only adopt the language of Oneness but continue to act in duality, the result will be just another instance of using form to avoid substantive change. Form is easily morphed to disguise true intent or actual motive. Language that discerns between form and substance will avoid such sleights of hand and permit us to construct substantive change that supports our journey toward Oneness.

Eleven

INSTITUTIONALIZED ONENESS: THE COMMUNITY MODEL IN CORRECTIONS®

Respect, being a contributing member, and honoring the integrity of the community are fundamental to the process.

Our old dualistic institutions are a choice we have made, not an inevitable outcome. When we intentionally build our institutions around the organizing principle of Oneness, it leads to harmony and order. A compelling example is found in a program created for jails and prisons called Community Model in Corrections®[66] (community model). It is an unconventional response to those who have committed crime—it uses only respectful means and, in doing so, it consistently achieves positive results, despite the participants' history of criminal conduct. It adds value to the whole.

The creators of the community model, Morgan Moss and Penny Patton, have extensive experience with treatment programs in correctional facilities. Time and again they saw the traditional treatment provided to inmates turn into a game in which the inmates ostensibly complied, while continuously trying to outwit the therapists. The inmates' wisdom and experience regarding their own recovery and improvement were systematically ignored. "They were convinced that if, instead, the inmates were shown how to form a pro-social, self-governing unit within the institution, and were empowered to offer mutual aid to one another, the anti-social culture that pervades so many correctional institutions could be transformed into a positive, adaptive community."[67] They set about creating a program organized to meet these goals.

Because the community model introduces a new culture in the institution, it must begin with full buy-in from the jail administration. The new culture will be one in which inmates are treated as "experts" on their own recovery and rehabilitation. They experience ownership, respect, dignity, and trust—the opposite of what is often the norm in our penal institutions.

The program officially begins when the inmates who have volunteered to participate are moved to a separate housing unit within the penal institution. While a typical penal housing unit is sterile and the furniture is bolted to the floor, in the community model, stacks of chairs are available for sitting in a circle in the community meeting area, where much of the work of building community and healing is done. A clock is hung high on the wall, and program materials are made available for the group to share.

When Patton and Moss first meet with a new group, they intentionally treat the entire group as a viable community, thus indirectly affirming that each participant deserves dignity and respect. Moss and Patton take care not to single out any individual participant for special attention, as this undermines the cohesion of the group. They avoid having volunteers come into the community who want to be do-gooders, treating the participants with sentimentality. Moss and Patton find sentimentality and brutality both to be harmful, each disempowering the recipient in its own way. They ward off anything that implies the inmates cannot do for themselves, or that little is expected of them.

At their first meeting with the community, they open by saying, "I think this group could become a community. What do you think?" In one particular women's group, Patton reports that for the first two sessions the women complained about the body odor of new female inmates who didn't have enough money to buy soap and shampoo in the canteen. They grumbled about forming a community that included women who stank. Patton's response was to consistently and patiently ask, "What can you do about this?"

By the third session, the women had an answer. Those who had a little extra money on the canteen books offered to purchase soap and shampoo so the group could present a small welcoming package to the new inmates who came in with no money—a solution everyone felt good about.

In a community model program, the participants solving their own problems is just one of the benefits. Specific activities are scheduled for twelve hours a day to facilitate the inmates taking a hard look at themselves, while experientially addressing problems together. This is the best means of promoting safety. They begin learning social skills for changing past conduct and transforming themselves internally. The philosophy and approach are related to the twelve steps found in Alcoholics Anonymous. Voluntary AA/NA groups are incorporated into the program. A wide variety of other groups is also offered, and as soon as possible, these groups are facilitated by the inmates themselves. Respect, being a contributing member, and honoring the integrity of the community are fundamental to the process.

Within the first few months, senior members who have been democratically elected by the group begin to oversee the daily activities of the new community. While jail rules are considered nonnegotiable, participants are offered certain basic community rules and the freedom to adopt guidelines that are in harmony with their particular cultural, emotional, and spiritual needs. This promotes the trust necessary for the participants to face the risk of deep-seated change.

Issues of program compliance, complacency, and destructive behavior are addressed in participant-led community meetings. By addressing matters of civility and working on recovery from addictive behaviors and self-limiting beliefs, they learn to consider new approaches. As the community matures, the sense of ownership and autonomy the participants develop leads to higher levels of motivation, participation, and responsibility. Negative behaviors are all but eliminated, and when they do arise, they are quickly resolved through this community process. Correctional officer concerns about suicides, contraband, assaults on staff, and inmate altercations are essentially nonexistent. Soon the community polices itself.

It is noteworthy that, in a mature community, the members routinely institute and enforce standards that are higher than security staff would attempt to enforce. In every program, the number of hearings for jail rule violations drops dramatically or they are virtually eliminated. Moreover, there is an absence of litigation, serious damage to property, rape, and gang-related violations. The safe and orderly operation of the institution is greatly enhanced, and the security needs of the institution are always met.

The depth of the emotional growth that occurs in these communities is reflected in the pain that is shared when staff are not present, for here it is safe to experience and express deep wounds that must be addressed in order for healing to occur. In the community model, members learn that giving consistent, truthful, and heartfelt feedback to one another builds trust and that unacceptable conduct impacts the whole community, not just the people involved in the conduct. This cultivates an awareness of the greater whole and a feeling of responsibility and accountability for the group experience. The program has been described as a process of re-parenting for those who grew up in dysfunctional environments.[68]

By consistently building a win-win context in which people can learn from their mistakes and conflicts are continuously addressed, each community forms a self-governing unit that is prepared to actively "habilitate" and heal its members. The participants build what Robert W. Fuller, author of *All Rise: Somebodies, Nobodies, and the Politics of Dignity,* calls a dignitarian community, an environment in which the dignity of everyone is protected and honored.[69]

Once the community becomes seasoned in the process, Moss, Patton, and their staff intentionally step aside and permit the community to run with little input from them. Their job becomes remaining alert to what is unfolding within the community and offering adjustments and the interventions needed to inspire self-reflection and cohesion. The goal is to help the participants create their own workable consensus. As the participants learn to tend and nurture this new culture, the preservation of the community is on solid ground.

In contrast, the traditional treatment context emphasizes professional authoritarianism while disempowering the inmates. This labor-intensive process involves writing treatment plans and diagnosing or enforcing other top-down processes, even when they are not necessary. For the non-severe emotionally disturbed inmate, the rigors of a full assessment can be harmful, especially when services are not available and assessments do not provide adequate emotional closure for the wounds that are revisited.

The extensive paperwork involved makes this approach expensive, with minimal return on investment. The emphasis placed on individual assessment and treatment plans gives the professionals the authority to decide what each inmate needs, but inadvertently encourages inmates to try to beat the system to get what they want. One member of a community model program reported that he had been under psychiatric care for years. In the traditional system, he became skilled at manipulating his psychiatrists while appearing to be compliant. In contrast, in the community model group, he faced thirty-five peers who knew his tricks, denial, and deception. He admitted, "I can't BS a room full of BS'ers."[70]

The traditional model often achieves only first-order change, limited to simple compliance to appease the hierarchy or be accepted into the group.[71] It typically addresses only the symptoms, not the solutions.

When the context of belonging and contribution is experienced and maintained, participants often achieve second-order change, change that is fundamental, internalized, and becomes reflected in maturity, awareness, wisdom, and generosity toward others. This happens without force or coercion. In a mature community, participants are more honest, generous, and compassionate, more accepting of responsibility for their own actions and for what happens within the community, than is the norm in outside society.

Mental health and substance abuse professionals already at an institution are considered to be part of the community model team, providing the critical mental health assessments and services that are actually needed. This is more effective, saving time and money, than trying to provide one-on-one or individual assessment or therapy for all the inmates, which too often fosters manipulation, enabling, and piles of files. In fact, participants in a mature community model often come to question medication and therapy for non-severe mental health issues and see them as a crutch.

When Moss and Patton first set up a community model program, some security staff doubted it would work, expecting that the anti-social or predatory inmates would take control. They derided the attempt, saying it was like turning the asylum over to the patients. By the time the first community model certificate ceremony took place, many staff members admitted they had been converted.

Fears that this type of program coddles inmates and fails to sufficiently punish them are unfounded. In a traditional penal institution, inmates spend hours sleeping, watching TV, playing mindless games, and learning how to better commit crime, while they are consumed with conflict among themselves and contempt toward the officers. Those programs offer nothing comparable to the many hours of intense behavioral, mental, emotional, and spiritual work that the community model offers.

Moss and Patton began developing this restorative model specifically for correctional institutions in 1999.[72] Experience has shown that, in addition to providing inmates the pro-social skills necessary to be contributing members of society, the program has a positive impact on the overall jail environment. The presence of a community model program increases the safe and orderly operation of the entire institution and improves the security of the community in which the institution is located.

As one would expect, upon release from jail, again being surrounded by people in the old mind-set makes it difficult to sustain the new norms and behavior. To support the change that has taken place, the former inmates meet weekly to reinforce the process they began in the community model program, a sort of jail alumni association. Taking what they have learned back to the street and to their communities often restores and improves offender-family relations. They come to value the paradox that, in order to keep what they have experienced, they must give it away.

A study of recidivism among those who experience a community model program was conducted at the South Side Regional Jail in Emporia, Virginia. The data indicate that recidivism rates are low for those who complete community model programs—less than 10 percent in the three years after release.[73] The track record for prisoners in traditional programs is dismal in comparison. A fifteen-state study found that, in only three years, more than two-thirds of those released were rearrested.[74] A recidivism rate of over 60 percent is the norm.

The objectives of the community model program are achieved at a fraction of the cost of traditional clinical treatment. Each such program (approximately fifty to sixty inmates) requires only part-time unlicensed staff to be on-site, and most of the on-site supervision occurs during the launch of the model.

This stands in stark contrast to the setup of traditional programs, some of which may have a couple of full-time licensed professionals serving as few as a dozen inmates at each institution. On the average, a community model program costs approximately one-fourth the cost of a traditional treatment program or therapeutic community. A documentary, *The Community Model in Corrections®*, is available at www.communitymodel.org.

Moss and Patton envision the day when community model principles are used in other realms of criminal law, such as reentry programs, probation, and parole, in problem-solving courts and social detox programs. They have designed a community model new entry program for those being released from jail or prison.

Replication

The success of the community model can be attributed in large part to the controlled environment the correctional facility provides. Under the right circumstances, however, that is not necessary. When there is an intense desire and the discipline to constantly, and without exception, act with love and forgiveness, individuals can replicate similar results, even outside a cloistered-type environment. It begins by disciplining the mind to be quiet, by being compassionate toward everything, even oneself, and having the will to hold personal desires in abeyance. By surrendering each thought, emotion, and deed to a higher power, personal will can be overcome.[75]

As the mind is progressively disciplined, David Hawkins describes what happens. At first, paragraphs and whole stories are released, then ideas and concepts. "As one lets go of wanting to own these thoughts, they no longer reach such elaboration and begin to fragment while only half formed. Finally it [is] possible to surrender the energy behind the very process of thinking itself before it even [becomes] a thought."[76]

To undertake a serious practice of mental discipline, one can begin by attending ten-day Vipassna meditation retreats taught by S. N. Goenka and his associates around the world.[77] These retreats are offered free of charge, being supported exclusively by voluntary donations made by the students. While these retreats usually take place outside penal institutions, a documentary about their use in a Kentucky prison called *Dhamma Brothers, East Meets West in the Deep South* gives insight into the teaching.[78]

The foundation on which the Community Model in Corrections® is built can serve as a source of inspiration when creating structures in any setting where the creation and maintenance of healthy human relations are key, such as schools, work environments, and places of worship. That this is possible is no longer in doubt.

Twelve

INSTITUTIONALIZED DUALITY:
THE STANFORD PRISON EXPERIMENT

An ecology of dehumanization is often cloaked in ideology that justifies the conduct as necessary to attain an ultimate goal.

Building an institutional structure around the disorganizing process of duality leads to disorder and insecurity, as demonstrated by a well-known experiment conducted by a group of social scientists in the early 1970s. The Stanford Prison Experiment, led by Philip Zimbardo, began as an undergraduate class study of the psychology of imprisonment. It was designed to differentiate between what people bring into a prison environment from what the prison environment brings out in the people who are there.[79] While not the intention, it demonstrated the essential elements of a dualistic system and its consequences.

For the experiment, a mock prison was set up in the basement of the university's psychology building, using a thirty-five-foot section of corridor to simulate a cell block. Three laboratory rooms were turned into six-by-nine-foot cells, complete with black steel-barred doors. A solitary confinement cell was set up in a closet.

The group advertised in local papers for male students willing to volunteer for the experiment. Out of seventy-five applicants, twenty-one were selected who tested as being the most normal and healthy based on a battery of psychological tests. Half of the group was randomly designated to serve as guards. These men were given uniforms and dark glasses, and charged with keeping order in the mock prison.

To heighten the reality of the experiment, Zimbardo arranged for members of the Palo Alto Police Department to simulate arrests and handcuff the experiment's prisoners in their homes, and bring them to the station house. There they were charged with a fictitious crime, fingerprinted, and blindfolded by the police before being taken to the mock prison. Upon arrival, they were stripped by those designated to be guards and given prison uniforms that had a number on the front and back, which would serve as their only identification.

The results were stark. The guards, some of whom had previously considered themselves pacifists, quickly exerted abusive control and imposed severe discipline on the prisoners. For instance, on the first night, the prisoners were awakened at two in the morning and made to do push-ups and other arbitrary tasks.

On the morning of the second day, the prisoners rebelled. They ripped the numbers off their uniforms and barricaded themselves in their cells. The reaction of the guards was to exert greater control. They stripped the prisoners, sprayed them with fire extinguishers, and threw the leader of the rebellion into solitary confinement. One guard described what developed as an atmosphere of terror, which became more abusive and sadistic as the experiment progressed.

Prisoners were made to march down the hallway in handcuffs with paper bags over their heads. The guards demeaned the prisoners and forced them to be abusive to each other. In a few short days, the guards withheld the prisoners' food, denied them bathroom privileges, some prisoners were forced to sleep on the bare floor, and most were punished with nudity and sexual humiliation. A guard later reported having been extremely creative in the forms of mental cruelty he devised.[80]

After thirty-six hours, one prisoner became hysterical and had to be released from the project. Four more were released due to extreme depression, crying, rage, and anxiety. Slated to last two weeks, the experiment was terminated after six days. Zimbardo reported that the scientists had not expected either the intensity of the change in conduct or the speed with which it happened.

After the experiment was over, one prisoner said: "I realize now that no matter how together I thought I was inside my head, my prisoner behavior was often less under my control than I realized." Another described feeling like he was losing his identity:

The person I call Clay, the person who volunteered to get me into this prison (because it was prison to me, it still is a prison to me, I don't regard it as an experiment or a simulation . . .) was distant from me, was remote, until finally I wasn't that person. I was 416. I was really my number and 416 was really going to have to decide what to do.[81]

In this environment of repression, those who believed they had unrestricted control over the others quickly fell into base, less than humane conduct. Those being controlled were reduced to coping or survival mode. If the abusive control had extended over a longer period of time, the prisoners might have been inclined to scheme until they either reversed roles and gained control of their surroundings, or they escaped, using any means available. If those strategies failed or were not accessible, another strategy would have been to relinquish all self-will to those in control.

The vengeance-seeking that drives such a system focuses on control, but it actually makes control difficult to maintain. The corrosive and self-destructive nature of this form of justice only escalates until it is brought into check by the norms inherent in the restorative model, such as respect, honesty, integrity, and trust.

Correctional institutions are unique in that the isolation of their closed environment heightens the conforming effect. Part of the success of the community model in corrections is that its participants are immersed in the experience of pro-social norms 24/7. The isolation of the Stanford Prison Experiment also contributed to how rapidly its participants conformed to its anti-social environment.

Many years after the Stanford Prison Experiment, Zimbardo wrote a book called *The Lucifer Effect: Understanding How Good People Turn Evil* in which he considered the larger ramifications of the college project. He attributed the descent of these normal, emotionally healthy college students into depravity to the cultivation of an ecology of dehumanization.[82] As he considered the larger perspective, he concluded that the most important lesson learned was that situations such as this are the outgrowth of systems that provide the necessary institutional support, authority, and resources for them to exist.

The torture and inhumane treatment perpetrated by otherwise normal American soldiers at the Abu Ghraib prison during the Iraq War is an example cited by Zimbardo of how an ecology of dehumanization turns good people into monsters. Another is the slaughter of more than five hundred Vietnamese women, children, and elderly men by American soldiers at My Lai during the Vietnam War. He cites many others. Zimbardo posits a question which, he notes, is rarely asked:

"Who or what made it happen that way?" Who had the power to design the behavioral setting and to maintain its operation in particular ways? Therefore, who should be held responsible for its consequences and outcomes? Who gets the credit for successes, and who is blamed for failures?[83]

Zimbardo points out that it is not always easy to pinpoint the culprits. An ecology of dehumanization is often cloaked in ideology that justifies the conduct as necessary to attain an ultimate goal. The ideology permits those up and down the chain of command to present destructive conduct as a highly valuable moral imperative, and many become involved in its implementation. As the ideology becomes widely accepted and opposition is silenced, the procedures are condoned, justified as reasonable and appropriate.[84] Sometimes we call such conduct *justice*.

Now a professor emeritus at Stanford University, Zimbardo recently said that, while all violence is composed of individual acts, the profession of psychology errs by not examining other forces that make up the whole. "Political, historical, cultural, legal and economic forces embed people in situations like Abu Ghraib, yet our justice, religious, health and psychiatric systems focus solely on the individual."[85] When we focus on individual guilt instead of all the forces at play, we cannot see the root of problems, find interests we have in common, or achieve the wellness of the whole. As a result, we all lose.

Good apples rot in a rotten barrel. Zimbardo also notes that turning the social model around to enhance positive acts can be effective in achieving desirable outcomes.[86] Just as Moss and Patton have found, a good barrel produces good apples. It is the environment that is often the deciding factor.

Preserving the Environment

Various restorative justice approaches to conflict resolution show us that a respectful and safe environment causes the people in it to become respectful, self-reliant, and healthy community members. It results in greater peace and a shared sense of justice among those involved. The Stanford Prison Experiment teaches us that destructive norms can be applied instead. They often are, while justice is reduced to nothing more than a measure of the teeth lost and the eyes blinded.

As we build institutions on the organizing principle of Oneness, the culture must be carefully nurtured. In the community model, for example, the environment is preserved by empowering the community to vote a person out for thirty days if he disrupts the culture by repeatedly violating its standards. On rare occasions the institution's staff have removed an offender, but only in immature communities not yet equipped to deal with serious infractions.

While this consequence might appear to be punishment, the end it seeks to achieve is different. It is done not to shame the offender, but to protect the culture and community. This difference changes the meaning of the removal, and its impact on the offender. Many of those removed from the community model immediately apply to return and come with a new commitment to live within its norms. In contrast, many who participated in the Stanford Prison Experiment are still scarred by that experience.

At the heart of the community model's transformative power is respect—for oneself, for others, for the community, and for the whole of life. Extending respect in the face of disrespect is one of the most disarming responses to attack possible. Even those whom we label criminals rise to exemplary standards when they are consistently extended respect in an environment where all are held to the same norms.

Realism Versus Illusions

The Community Model in Corrections® and the Stanford Prison Experiment are examples of the mental structures of Oneness and duality on a limited scale. The U.S. reaction to 9/11 provides lessons learned on the worldwide stage.

A few weeks before he left office in January 2009, President George W. Bush recalled the outpouring of love and support for the United States in the days immediately after the attack:

> [J]ust a few weeks after September the 11th, 2001—I said that America would always remember the signs of support from our friends. . . . I remember the American flag flying from every fire truck in Montreal, Canada. I remember children kneeling in silent prayer outside our embassy in Seoul. I remember baseball players in Japan observing moments of silence. I remember a sign handwritten in English at a candlelight vigil in Beijing that read, "Freedom and justice will not be stopped."[87]

This unconditional support did not last long. It began to wane around the time President Bush indicated the path his administration would take when he spoke at the Pentagon on September 17, 2001. Toward Osama bin Laden, he demanded vengeance: "I want justice. And there's an old poster out West, as I recall, that said, 'Wanted: Dead or Alive.'"

When he was asked for clarification, he reiterated:

> I just remember, all I'm doing is remembering when I was a kid I remember that they used to put out there in the old West, a wanted poster. It said: "Wanted, Dead or Alive." All I want, and America wants him brought to justice. That's what we want.[88]

When Bush demanded bin Laden be delivered to him, dead or alive, he ignored the lessons taught by earlier leaders like Buddha, Genghis Khan, Jesus, Hitler, Mahatma Gandhi, Stalin, Martin Luther King Jr., and Saddam Hussein about how

Oneness and duality play out. Attacking one's enemies does not make one revered in the annals of history. Those who forgive are revered.

Soon thereafter, Afghanistan was bombed in retaliation for permitting Al Qaeda to train within its borders. The attack and occupation of Iraq followed, ostensibly to protect the United States against its weapons of mass destruction which were later confirmed not to exist. By then, the image of the United States was sorely tarnished, and it was difficult to find allies to join our coalition of the willing to fight in Iraq.

We failed in not considering the whole, including our own misdeeds. In the Arab world, they have not forgotten that the United States helped assassinate Iran's democratically elected president in 1953 when he wanted to nationalize some of the nation's oil reserves. Without healing that wound, how could justifying the attack on Iraq as building democracy be heard as anything but hypocrisy? Yet during the Bush years, suggesting that aspects of U.S. involvement in the Middle East could have fueled the attack on the United States was scorned by those in control as pandering to the enemy, thus discouraging analysis and reflection.

The lessons of the Iraq War have been costly. Might does not make right. Political scientist Francis Fukuyama points out that imbalance in might must be addressed for balance to be restored:

> [T]he United States can affect many countries around the world without their being able to exercise a reciprocal degree of influence on the United States. This is most glaringly obvious in the military realm, where the United States can change a regime 8,000 miles away. But the disparity exists in a host of other domains, as when an agricultural subsidy or change in trade rules can wipe out an entire sector in a developing country's economy. Few

trust the United States to be sufficiently benevolent or wise to use its one-sided influence for everyone's benefit without the subjection of American power to more formal constraints.[89]

While he did not talk about it in these terms, Fukuyama is describing foreign policy that is grounded in duality: us versus them, win-lose, attack is how we must maintain control to serve our interests. This approach leads to distrust, breakdown, and needless death. However, the implication of what Fukuyama says is that if the United States shifts its policies toward Oneness, the impact will not only affect its citizens, but also the entire world. Such change is emerging.

After hard lessons learned in Afghanistan and Iraq, the need for a more holistic approach has been expressed in the 2008 edition of the army operations manual. Military leaders like Army Colonel H. R. McMaster, one of the military leaders in the Iraq War, recognized the flaws in an exaggerated faith in military technology, while undervaluing measures that help repair the breach. The new operations manual promotes the mission of stabilizing war-torn countries to equal importance with defeating opponents on the battlefield.

This is a step toward Oneness, and the army reasonably anticipates resistance to the new policy until a new culture that is supportive replaces the old mind-set.[90] President Barack Obama may be cultivating such a culture when he uses a more inclusive language and considers more pieces of the whole.

Thirteen

PRACTICING ONENESS

As we let go of the forms that no longer serve us, we find that the dream of discovering a benevolent universe is not a dream after all, because we possess the power to create that benevolence!

Can Oneness be achieved in the here and now? Not instantly, perhaps, but more and more people are choosing to incorporate the organizing principle of Oneness into their lives. A compelling example is Thomas Ann Hines, a Texas woman whose son was shot to death by a young man in a carjacking attempt. She recounts that for the first seven years after her son's death, she was angry and prayed for the murderer to die. Then she came to realize that she was killing herself with her prayers for vengeance.

Thomas Ann entered a restorative justice program called Transformative Justice and began a yearlong process that included her son's murderer, as both prepared to meet one another. In correspondence prior to their meeting, he warned her not to expect him to say he was sorry for what he had done. Nonetheless, this year laid the foundation for the two of them to see the murder of her son within a larger context than they had when it was committed.

When the day to meet arrived, Thomas Ann could not imagine what words she would say to the man who had taken so much from her. As they were seated at a small table, under the watchful eye of prison guards, she began to tell him about her son, the things they had done together, how precious he—her only child—had been to her. Her heartfelt honesty began to disarm the man to whom she spoke.

He listened. "I didn't realize . . . how stupid it was," he began to say. He confessed that he had given no thought to any of it, before or since that fateful night. This process of honest sharing led both the perpetrator and Thomas Ann to temporarily set judgment aside.

As their talk was coming to an end, Thomas Ann heard a voice in her head say, "Reach out and offer your hand to him." Her reply, in her head, was, "No, that's the hand that held the gun." The voice again said, "Reach out and offer your hand to him." She thought in response, "I can't do it by myself."

Thomas Ann closed her eyes and bowed her head, then extended her hand across the table. The man who had ended her son's life reached out and took her hand. In this moment of connectedness, he put his head down on their joined hands and wept. Within them both, there was a shift beyond the bodily level to the place where forgiveness is the only choice one would consider and instantaneous healing occurs. The bitterness, even the misunderstanding, the distance between these two human beings from vastly different worlds, vanished. In seeing the humanity in each other, they knew they had certain interests in common. Where forgiveness has occurred, there must be Oneness among people, for nothing remains to keep them apart.

After this meeting, Thomas Ann's life went from one consumed by darkness and self-pity, a small life at best, to one of giving, passion, and commitment, teaching others the healing effect of forgiveness that she learned. She began speaking in prisons, spending many hours talking to inmates about what happens to the victims of their misdeeds. Experiencing her defenselessness and nonjudgment, many heard her and understood. The remorse that transforms behavior is far more likely to be felt under these circumstances than in the face of judgment and condemnation.

Before their meeting, the young man had been a problem prisoner, having accrued nearly 150 major violations while in prison. Since their meeting, he has had only a few minor violations. While some people may forever label him as a murderer for the wrong he committed, in a few fleeting moments, this mother's forgiveness brought him to a commitment to a different way of being. Each day, Thomas Ann now prays that no harm will come to him. Out of tragedy came transformation. Is this not how justice should be?

After her son's murder, Thomas Ann's first response was to feel angry. Anger denies that peace exists or that it is even desirable. Forgiveness permitted Thomas Ann to release her anger, and with that, she experienced peace. In forgiving her son's murderer, she found her own healing, and facilitated his.

Forgiveness led Thomas Ann, in time, to a place of knowing that there was nothing to forgive—that all is in Divine Order. She has come to believe that, on some level, her son willingly gave his life so that she might live, not in the dark life she had known, but in the light of love. This is not to say that her life is now pure bliss or that she does not miss her son. It simply means one source of pain and preoccupation has been replaced with peace, making way for other problems to be addressed as they arise. She now knows how to achieve such peace, and is teaching others. The winners are Thomas Ann, the man to whom she reached out, and every individual whose life they touch with their new understanding

A Cry for Love Replaces Evil

Why are acts of forgiveness such as Thomas Ann's less common than those of vengeance? As long as we believe that the first step is to judge the wrong done, we are focusing on the past, making it harder to turn to the future, or even be present to the now. In this mind-set, it seems like forgiveness requires that the past be overlooked, and that we must give up something valuable while getting nothing in return. Being told that inflicting punishment will secure compliance, we believe that more harm is necessary and we cannot see that, as a systematic institutionalized approach, it is neither logical nor effective.

For many offenders, being judged guilty leads to a defensive mode. Many rationalize the harm they inflicted and project blame upon the very ones whom they harmed so that everyone involved is caught in the circular trap of dual morality, seeing themselves as innocent victims and the other as evil. In the process, judgment stands in the way of forgiveness and guilt trumps remorse, making peace and well-being unattainable.

The path to healing requires that, from the outset, we look beyond the error committed by the offender to the truth about the offender's humanity, as well as our own. Love is so prevalent and powerful that wrongful acts must be a failure to comprehend Oneness, a mistaken belief in duality. This understanding opens the space needed to see the error as a cry for love, so we need not undo a layer of judgment to reach forgiveness. We may proceed directly to answering the other's cry for love by extending our love to them, and all benefit. We are commanded to love one another because our peace and joy lies in the love we hold for others.

Some falter at the thought of forgiveness, demanding that remorse come before forgiveness is even considered. In Oneness, forgiveness gives rise to remorse, and remorse gives rise to forgiveness, a causality so circular that neither precedes the other. Regardless of whether forgiveness or remorse sparks the process, the outcome will be mutually beneficial. When we focus on our shared humanity, as Thomas Ann eventually did, this is when miracles appear in our lives.

When we forgive, we are not condoning wrongdoing. The goal of forgiveness is not to enable a dysfunctional situation to persist—it is to restore balance and harmony. Intervention aimed at stopping the harm, when done in the spirit of preserving the peace and harmony of the community, not in seeking vengeance and retribution, enables the offender to see things differently, to feel remorse, and to choose anew. After all, it is also his community.

These circumstances are vastly different from the world of duality, where no real healing occurs for the parties involved. There, the offender is the object of blame and revenge. An admission of responsibility makes him even more likely to experience retaliation, as he has proven the case against himself. Restoration to the community is often limited to privileged citizens, those who are well connected or rich enough to buy influence. Lacking the broader context of Oneness, many who are affected by the offender—often even the victim—are left outside of the process, unheard. In duality, retribution is placed above healing and building a cohesive community.

There are many examples of forgiveness leading to spiritual transformation for both the victim and the offender. In Azim Khamisa's book, *Azim's Bardo: A Father's Journey from Murder to Forgiveness,* he describes how he reconciled with the teenage California gang member who murdered his son, Tariq. Soon after Tariq's death, Khamisa set up the Tariq Khamisa Foundation to help potential gang members find themselves before they harmed others. First, he invited the murderer's grandfather, Ples Felix, to join him in this effort. In time, however, Khamisa knew his healing depended on forgiving the murderer. He pursued this, met with him in prison, and both Khamisa and the young man found healing in their reconciliation.

Khamisa now devotes much of his time to breaking the epidemic of youth violence by teaching these young people about forgiveness, self-responsibility, and the importance of becoming peacemakers. As soon as the man who murdered Khamisa's son is released from prison, he has a job waiting for him in the Tariq Khamisa Foundation. He will be given the task of reaching out to young gang members, teaching them forgiveness and reconciliation.

The mental structures of Oneness and duality are equally applicable in the public arena where millions of people are involved. History books are full of such examples. After the Civil War, Abraham Lincoln wanted the simplest of terms for the surrender of the Confederate army: that they lay down their arms and go home so this nation could heal. He also wanted former slaves who were literate to be given the vote as a salve on the wounds of slavery. That surely reflected an understanding of the importance of setting aside the past in the interest of healing and peace, as Oneness requires.

Unfortunately, after Lincoln's assassination, those who ended up with the reins of government in the South possessed the far more common inclination. They were determined that vengeance be sought and former slaves be given as few rights as possible. As a result, even now, for a surprising number of southerners, the wounds left by that war remain unhealed—a demonstration of how vengeance and healing are mutually exclusive.

During the Great Depression, Franklin Delano Roosevelt saw in the people a power to be harnessed for the common good. Rather than pitting one economic segment of the population against another, as could have been done, he built on the interests that everyone shared by putting those without jobs to work with subsidized employment. He established programs that provided a safety net for those at the bottom that those at the top helped finance. As a new, more stable, economic order was put into place, the nation recovered and everyone won. The crisis was defeated—another example of the power of Oneness.

The Treaty of Versailles Versus the Marshall Plan

What happened at the end of World War I and World War II provides a concrete example of how duality and vengeance lead to more war, while Oneness and forgiveness lead to peace. It shows that the interplay between forgiveness and remorse is applicable even on the largest of scales.

The stage for World War I was set by the late 1800s. Changes in the balance of power in Europe had set in motion a downward spiral that encompassed much of Europe. The powder keg exploded with the assassination of Archduke Franz Ferdinand of Austria-Hungary in 1914, and war erupted.

In 1917, President Woodrow Wilson told the U.S. Congress that a Declaration of War against Germany was necessary in order that the world "be made safe for democracy." But at the end of World War I, when Germany had been defeated, the Allies chose not to render support to the fledgling liberal democracy established by the 1919 German constitution. They instead sought retribution. The Treaty of Versailles demanded reparations from Germany for the destruction its war machine had caused. It forbade Germany to have a military and paved the way for later French occupation of a portion of its land. This hindered Germany's recovery and left its people angry and in pain.

Hitler offered them an answer: more vengeance. He then continued the downward spiral, taking fear and control to the extreme by killing millions of Jews, gypsies, homosexuals, the mentally impaired, and others, as well as the thousands of soldiers who died in the war. The whole world was sucked into the violence, Hitler's capitulation coming only when his soldiers could no longer fight his wars. By taking his own life, Hitler escaped seeing his deeds, and those of his henchmen, exposed to the light. This is the mind-set of duality.

But Hitler's downward spiral was not predetermined. The Allies' need for vengeance helped build the pulpit for Hitler's sermons of mass murder. The Allies could have chosen, instead, to support the fledgling democracy in Germany and helped rebuild the nation, despite its prior transgressions. This could have avoided the hardship and bitterness that gave Hitler the platform he needed to organize, and then carry out, what amounted to barbarism.

At the end of World War II, aid offered to all the war-torn nations of Europe, including Germany, demonstrates how different the outcome can be when vengeance is relinquished in favor of restoration and reconciliation. The United Nations Relief and Rehabilitation Administration helped millions of World War II refugees and was instrumental in achieving European postwar recovery. Through the Marshall Plan, the United States spent billions of dollars on economic and technical assistance to help the recovery of the European countries that shared our system of representative democracy and free market economy, which included postwar West Germany. In a relatively short time, the economy of Western Europe had grown beyond prewar levels. Only West Germany lagged behind, but eventually it too caught up and excelled.

The Marshall Plan helped establish an environment that promoted European integration by reducing tariff trade barriers and setting up continental-wide institutions to coordinate the economy. This integration was continued by the European Economic Community—now the European Union—that formed after World War II and includes former foes. The EU serves as another example of setting aside anger in the interest of building peace and security.

The United States instituted a program similar to the Marshall Plan in Japan, the other major World War II enemy. By joining the Allies in stopping the bloodshed, then commencing programs of restoration and conflict resolution—without seeking retribution—the

United States helped its former foes to recover. Out of remorse in Germany and Japan arose a strong desire to be good neighbors. Democracy flourished in both countries, and they became strong U.S. allies. Germany became a leader in the European Union, and the small nation of Japan became one of the world's strongest economies.

Only in laying aside the thirst for vengeance was remorse on the part of former foes made safe, the wounds of the past healed, and peace restored. Imagine the world that would emerge if even a small number of policy makers understood the power that lies within this approach.

Nonviolence, Even Nonresistance

What about statutes that say it is not a crime to harm others when an individual uses what the law defines as "reasonable and necessary force for self-defense or the defense of others"?[91]

This leads to what, for some people, is a difficult question: To apply the organizing principle of Oneness, must we give up self-defense when we need it to protect ourselves from harm? This question usually assumes that self-defense entails violence answering violence, but is this necessarily the case?

Think of how impervious the British Empire in India appeared to be before Mahatma Gandhi and his devotees used nonviolent civil disobedience instead of violence or revenge. Gandhi won without firing a single shot because, when the British used their weapons against defenseless Indians, they lacked moral legitimacy; it hurt the British more than it hurt their adversaries. When confronted with determined nonviolent civil disobedience that was not going to stop, the British were left with no option but to return India to its native people.

The U.S. civil rights movement is another example. Inspired by Gandhi's successful movement and led by Martin Luther King

Jr., a band of young African Americans trained in nonviolent civil disobedience ended legalized racial segregation in the southern United States through the force of will, not the force of arms. When these peaceful marchers were attacked by police dogs, water hoses, and clubs, the power of their nonresistance immediately discredited their attackers and led to segregation's demise.

After years of civil strife in a racially divided nation, the Truth and Reconciliation trials in South Africa under the chairmanship of Desmond Tutu showed how truth is more easily discovered when the heart is open and the reward is to be forgiven. Instead of asking that their tormentors be punished, as an eye-for-an-eye justice would have it, there were moments during some trials when victims of terrible atrocities felt a shift, connected to something greater than themselves, and spontaneously embraced the perpetrators. Other nations torn with civil strife have instituted Truth and Reconciliation trials in one form or another, demonstrating there is a better way.

It was the practice of nonresistance that enabled Buddhist monks in Myanmar (Burma) to chant lovingkindness meditations while soldiers smashed their heads against the walls of their monasteries in October 2007. They were showing the soldiers that they could not hurt them—their bodies are secondary to who they are—and that they held nothing against their attackers, just as Jesus had done centuries earlier. This is the ultimate meaning of "turn the other cheek." To do otherwise is to choose duality over Oneness. This episode caused many people around the world to sympathize with the plight of the people living under that nation's dictator, General Than Shwe. It put his cruelty in the spotlight, delegitimized his regime, and weakened his support internationally.

To hold a grievance, to hate or attack, keeps us bound by the chains of duality and breaks our connection to Oneness. That is why people around the world did not empathize with the soldiers of Myanmar who were attacking the monks, or the police in Selma, Alabama, beating young African Americans. Their attacks seemed to split them off from the rest of us; we did not want to be connected with their deeds. The monks and young black Americans, however, immediately opened our hearts and called to us—they reminded us of who we are. Their courage, integrity, and commitment continue to inspire us.

When the leaders of a nonviolent movement apply the principle of Oneness, they are able to win the support of the people and weaken the loyalty of those who serve political forces wedded to duality. In so doing, they wield a power that can defeat entrenched dualistic structures. Some see nonviolent action and nonresistance as passive, weak responses. Gandhi, however, called nonviolence the greatest force at the disposal of mankind. He said it is "mightier than the mightiest weapon of destruction devised by the ingenuity of man."[92]

The virtue of nonviolence (not harming others) and nonresistance (not returning the attack of those who are attacking you) has been taught for centuries. Hinduism teaches that nonresistance is the highest virtue, that when someone has reached perfection, nonresistance is a spontaneous outpouring of his experience of God. But it also teaches that using free will to give up resistance is only possible if one is capable of resistance, and only then is it a virtue.[93] Otherwise, it can be a vice. For example, if a person feels victimized by not being heard, refusing to speak can be a form of psychological resistance or a passive-aggressive way of counterattacking. This is not to be confused with nonresistance.

In Taoism, this peaceful approach is called nonaggressive strength. Lao Tsu writes:

A skillful leader does not use force. A skillful fighter does not feel anger.

A skillful master does not engage the opponent.
A skillful employer remains low.

This is called the power in not contending.
This is called the strength to employ others.
This is called the highest emulation of Nature.[94]

Lao Tsu believed that the most capable leaders are not aggressive and have no need to prove themselves again and again. They are humble and act subtly and with composure. Events unfold naturally when the skillful leader uses compassion, not overt means, to organize others to achieve a collective end.

We know that Buddha unequivocally taught his followers to practice nonresistance, even in the face of harm. He said:

> If villainous bandits were to carve you limb from limb with a two-handled saw, even then the man that should give way to anger would not be obeying my teaching. Even then be it your task to preserve your hearts unmoved, never to allow an ill word to pass your lips, but always to abide in compassion and good-will, with no hate in your hearts, enfolding in radiant thoughts of love the bandit (who tortures you) and proceeding thence to enfold the whole world in your radiant thoughts of love, thoughts great, vast and beyond measure, in which no hatred is or thought of harm.[95]

What is to be gained from this response? This simple parable suggests an answer. A warrior general besieged a Buddhist monk. "Do you not see who I am?" the general shouted, brandishing his sword. "I have the might to kill you." The monk calmly looked at him and replied, "Sir, do you not see who I am?

I have the power to let you." In the end, instead of killing the monk, the general converted to the beliefs that made the monk so powerful.

The Christian Lesson

Many Christians are taught that, in certain circumstances, it is just to resort to violence. Intellectually, this seems quite rational, but it is not a belief that is supported by the teachings of Jesus. In the Sermon on the Mount, Christ told his followers that an eye for an eye was the old way, but he came to teach a new way. He began by describing the old law that sanctioned retributive justice, and then described what he came to teach us. He said,

> Don't resist violence! If you are slapped on one cheek, turn the other too.
>
> If you are ordered to court, and your shirt is taken from you, give your coat too.
>
> If the military demand that you carry their gear for a mile, carry it two.
>
> Give to those who ask, and don't turn away from those who want to borrow.
>
> There is a saying, "Love your friends and hate your enemies."
>
> But I say: Love your enemies! Pray for those who persecute you!
>
> In that way you will be acting as true sons of your Father in Heaven. For he gives his sunlight to both the evil and the good, and sends rain on the just and on the unjust too.

If you love only those who love you, what good is that? Even scoundrels do that much.

If you are friendly only to your friends, how are you different from anyone else? Even the heathen do that.

But you are to be perfect, even as your Father in Heaven is perfect.[96]

In case we didn't understand his message, the response of Christ to his persecution and crucifixion is a compelling demonstration of what nonresistance means. It's easy to love those who think and look like us, or give us love in return. But this does not release us from duality. When we love our enemies, the love we feel is not due to the kindness of our adversaries, their supportive nature, or what we stand to gain from the encounter. Rather, when we love our enemies, we know the love we experience is fundamentally who we are.[97]

When we compare the static mentality of minds trapped in duality to the spontaneous and insightful minds of Oneness, we can understand how, for those thinking dualistically, extending love to one's enemies makes no sense. When people are conditioned to see attack and war as necessary reactions to fear and separation, societies are chained to duality and limited to the tools of control and force. They are misguided by the inconsistent standards of dual morality.

The more we come to understand Oneness, however, the more war becomes the strange trafficking in grievances necessary to justify war and the calls for righteous revenge to sustain it. Neither side knows itself nor sees its so-called enemy as an expression of the Creator, so blame and shame are traded back and forth as the grievances increase with each exchange. Neither group sees that the anger it projects at the other is harming its own members, or that dropping bombs violates the law that we extend love to one another, a law that assures our own safety.

While most war memorials glorify war without accounting for the cost, the Vietnam War Memorial is an exception. This memorial is especially compelling because it is honest; the cost of that war is not glossed over. The names of the American men and women who paid the ultimate cost are inscribed in the black marble, and they elicit deeply felt sorrow.

Monuments and medals are often used to glorify war and gloss over its destructiveness. Each time our president distributes medals won in war, we might ask the president, "Why did you choose war to begin with? Why did you not find other means to address your grievances? They do exist. Why did you not call these men and women to perform magnificent acts of kindness, and then honor them for that success?"

We need, however, to proceed thoughtfully. Experience teaches us that change must not come too rapidly, for that gives rise to more fear. We cannot suddenly abolish the right to use force in self-defense or dismantle our national defense establishment overnight. To many, such a prospect feels like being denied their only lifeline to survival in the face of a serious threat.

Fundamental beliefs change through an evolutionary process. As Oneness emerges as reality, violence naturally becomes less acceptable and nonviolence becomes an easier choice. Ultimately, we realize that self-defense begins with a community norm that makes harming anyone, by anyone, a taboo.

We Are the Creators of Benevolence

History provides many examples of a better way. Mahatma Gandhi's independence movement, Martin Luther King Jr.'s civil rights movement, the Marshall Plan, and the Truth and Reconciliation trials of South Africa are but a few.

In the face of such compelling evidence, how can we deny that the principle of Oneness works and organizing around duality does not? Have our attacks and threats of attack made the world safe? Do we rest assured that we are making the world a better place for future generations? Or, despite the huge investment made in our defense systems, are we still insecure, still fearful of seen and unseen enemies?

There are those who will call our attention to the atrocities in the world and ask, how can we not want revenge? Over two hundred million people died in wars and genocides in the last century alone, and few are rushing to forgive Hitler, Stalin, and Mao for the murder of millions of Jews, Russians, and Chinese.

What these atrocities bear witness to is the dismal world of duality—the mistaken belief in separation. It leads us to see attack as the only means of defense, to see victory in taking from others all they have, including life, and even to blame the victims for the avengers' vengeance and greed.

Through logic, we can deduce that peace and security are not only possible when we apply the principle of Oneness, they are inevitable. The same universal laws that give rise to endless cycles of war and destruction when we choose duality also guarantee that peace and security will arise when Oneness is the principle we choose instead. The principle stands: when you attack another, you attack yourself; when you harm others, you self-destruct.

Doing unto others as you would have them do unto you is the principle that assures a new and safer world. As we let go of the forms that no longer serve us, we find that the dream of discovering a benevolent universe is not a dream after all, because we possess the power to create that benevolence!

Fourteen

CONDITIONS ARE RIPE FOR CHANGE

Not only is another world possible, she is on her way.
On a quiet day, I can hear her breathing. —Arundhati Roy

The old system is again in a cycle of instability. The world's population is aging,[98] an information revolution is fueling productivity while eliminating jobs,[99] climate change is reaching a crisis point, and the loss of biodiversity is proceeding at alarming speed.[100] Monetary instability in diverse parts of the world reflects the interdependence and destabilizing effect of global markets.[101] Futurist Peter Russell has predicted that "[o]ver the next twenty years, as much change will happen in the world as has occurred over the past 200 years."[102]

This time, the revolutionary conditions falling into place are building the bridge from duality to Oneness. As this revolution occurs, new structures that are consistent with the organizing principle of Oneness will arise with greater ease. Evidence that such a megatrend has already commenced spans the field of science, local institutions, and beyond.

Cyberspace

The science of quantum physics is redefining our relationship with the universe and with one another. In the collective consciousness, there is a growing recognition that we are each an interconnected and interdependent aspect of an integral whole—not separate and distinct parts of a fragmented whole.

Take, for example, the fact that physical location no longer separates us as it used to. I remember waiting in the meeting place at Heathrow Airport for my sisters who were arriving on later flights, that being the rudimentary way we had to find each other. The meeting place has been rendered obsolete by cell phones and GPS (global positioning systems) that permit us to inform each other of our location from moment to moment. Now, sitting in the airport, or even in the jungle, we can communicate by e-mail over the Internet as our messages are transmitted via satellites far above the Earth.

Information systems are the backbone of major structural change, and we now have the most efficient means of transmitting information ever envisioned. Most of the world is now connected in cyberspace, as information courses around the planet, even to remote areas of the globe. The Internet and cellular phones are building a gigantic new system for communication without boundaries, unrestricted by national or physical borders and largely beyond governmental control.

Citizens are using this system to transfer information to the bottom, informing grassroots groups about the need for strategic change and how to achieve it. Bloggers demand honesty and transparency where it is lacking. Web-based resources like Wikipedia, YouTube, Twitter, and Facebook fundamentally change how we share ideas and become informed. The Internet is having more than a ripple effect; it is a torrent carrying change forward.

We have adapted well to ubiquitous Internet service, but because our consciousness is shifting from separation to connectedness, this is only the beginning. Location awareness and location-based services that permit us to network with virtually any mobile device are transforming how we define and use space. A school used to be a physical location in the neighborhood. While this may still be the case, it may also be wherever one's computer happens to be. Even how we define a computer is being revised. It can now be something you put in your pocket or an automobile accessory, ever ready to access or share information with others, connecting us with the whole in a way previously unimagined.

Technological innovation compels us to expand our minds to include a new vision of architecture that bridges the gap between virtual space and physical space. One can now envision offices in open spaces, even outdoors, where multiple distractions replace the controlled environment of the common cubicle.[103] How will this impact the design of office equipment, office attire, how we supervise employees, and even how we design our cities?

How will the new technology affect the options we have for responding to crime or maintaining social order? How can it be used to further unitive justice? To successfully face the future, these are the types of questions that must be asked, and answered. The possibilities seem limited only by our imaginations and the frontiers of the technology made possible by quantum physics.

This is disrupting belief systems as old as humankind, but affirming ancient teachings about our Oneness that are to be found in all the major world religions. It disproves the duality-based religious doctrines and secular policies of separation that legitimize punitive justice, attack, and even war, leaving these widespread beliefs unsupported.

More and more people want solutions that reflect Oneness and make everyone winners, not outcomes that are fragmented, divisive, and temporary. A grassroots movement demanding Oneness cannot be far behind.

Structural Design

How we envision the structures in which we live, work, and play reflects how we see ourselves in the world. The concept of how we design these structures is evolving. During the Industrial Age, profitable and manageable uniformity was the goal, with little regard for the larger context. Unlimited material resources were assumed, and aesthetics were seen as an imposed design feature. In that paradigm, design decisions were made based on immediate utility and profit, independent of ecological or long-term considerations.

Sustainable design arose in response to the negative consequences of the earlier approach. Consideration of the complexity and uniqueness of ecosystems is becoming a priority, with special emphasis on local conditions. In the sustainable model, nature is central. Layers of elements—individual parts, networks, and the ecological whole—are given consideration. Green architecture, recycling, and Earth Day grew out of the sustainable design movement.

The next phase, ecological design, places greater emphasis on the wholeness of the system. The visible elements—the buildings, the land, the community—are taken into consideration, but so are the invisible elements—the laws, the traditions, the values of the people. They are seen as one all-encompassing living process to be considered in the design. The eco village movement is an example of this design approach. While ecological design is still cutting edge, an even more advanced design is being envisioned.

Regenerative design[104] carries us forward, seeking to access a new level of consciousness that acknowledges we are secondary agents of creation in the manifest realm. It sees living systems as purposeful, not random, and nature as intelligent, alive, self-organizing, and participatory. Recognizing we are part of nature, it asks how we can live in the forest so that both the forest and humans thrive, eliminating the human-versus-nature duality. It incorporates sacred geometry, circles, spirals, and the Fibonacci sequence into the design, creating resonance between the forms of nature and the form of the man-made structure.

Holographic organization is a term being used when universal principles are fully incorporated into institutional design. Some restorative justice programs, including the Community Model in Corrections® described in chapter 11, approach this level. This is what it means to be humans living in Oneness.

Conscious Capitalism

Even the old unconscious version of capitalism, grounded in duality, is giving way to the rise of conscious capitalism. In her book *Megatrends 2010,* Patricia Aburdene details how trends in society, economics, and spirituality are reshaping capitalism holistically.[105] Forces such as the rise of spirituality among CEOs, executives, and employees; socially responsible investment firms that limit their mutual fund holdings to corporations that demonstrate awareness; shareholder activism demanding corporate social responsibility; and the activism of consumers speaking through where their dollars are spent are forcing businesses to move toward Oneness and away from the old focus on profit and shareholder interest that disregard collateral costs.

Aburdene describes how "Divine Presence" is spilling into business, leading spiritual CEOs and senior executives in companies as diverse as Redken and Hewlett-Packard to transform their companies. She provides evidence that Oneness-oriented businesses are, in fact, more profitable in the long run than those based on greed and self-interest, and often in the short run as well.

Some companies are espousing peace. The Peace Company, under the stewardship of President Kimberly King, is a for-profit corporation that exclusively offers products and services that help cultivate a new culture of peace. The Forgiveness Project at Stanford University has shown businesses how effective forgiveness can be as a tool to increase employee satisfaction and productivity.

Bernard Lietaer, an international expert on money systems, also sees major change brewing for capitalism. He asserts that our consciousness about money is going to have to change as much in the next twenty years as it has over the past five thousand years.[106] The economic destabilization that commenced in 2007 and reached the crisis point in 2008–2009 has created urgency for change in long-entrenched economic structures.

Corporations have served a particularly important function in the modern world. Capitalism, as we know it, would not exist without them. Many people fail to realize that a corporation is not a physical structure, but rather a legal concept set up pursuant to state statutes and court decisions that, in essence, has no existence beyond that. While the original intent was to limit these unique entities to serving the common good, that purpose quickly morphed into privately owned institutions designed to maximize the owners' profit.

The source of corporate existence in state statutes means that their continued existence and the form it takes are subject to political will. Even corporations can evolve from dualistic institutions to again serving the common good, as was originally intended, or at least doing the rest of us no harm. There are varieties of capitalism[107] and varieties of corporations to choose among. We now have new tools to assess which are the best choices to create the world that will permit us to thrive, and perhaps are necessary for us to survive.

Peacebuilding

The academic study of war is a long-standing tradition. To study peace instead of war is revolutionary. In the last decade, academic training in peace studies has been growing at lightning speed.

For example, the Center for Justice and Peacebuilding at Eastern Mennonite University in Harrisonburg, Virginia, opened in 1994. It has grown to include graduate studies in Conflict Transformation, the Summer Peacebuilding Institute, and a program in Strategies for Trauma Awareness and Resilience.

Now over 250 U.S. colleges and universities offer degrees in peacebuilding and dispute resolution, representing a sea change in how to resolve conflict. Columbia University has the Saltzman Institute of War and Peace Studies and, at its teachers college, the Peace Education Center. Cornell University has the Peace Studies Program. The University of Colorado, the University of Missouri, the University of North Texas, and Colgate University also have peace programs, to name a few.

Academia has also instituted peace journalism, a new discipline that encourages conflict analysis and a nonviolent response in media reports. The institutionalization of peace studies is supported by other academic disciplines that are moving toward a wholeness perspective, such as biology seeing cooperation, not competition, as the fundamental means to human survival.

Even an overt attempt to move government in the direction of Oneness and peace is under way. The peace movement includes an active citizen effort led by Marianne Williamson to establish a Department of Peace within the U.S. executive branch.

Religion

Peace and ecology are being emphasized with less reticence and greater frequency in religion. Some of the older Christian denominations, such as the Quakers, the Mennonites, and the Brethren with long-standing traditions in nonviolence and pacifism, share a new pride in the wisdom of their traditions.

A major shift is also occurring among conservative Christians. Jim Wallis describes in his book *The Great Awakening*[108] how the religious right has lost influence by focusing on a few wedge issues, like abortion and same-sex marriage. These conservative Christians are more likely to vote based on issues of social justice like climate change, Darfur, and poverty now than ever before. Nicholas Kristof wrote in a *New York Times* opinion piece that evangelicals have "turned almost 180 degrees. Today, many evangelicals are powerful internationalists and humanitarians."[109] Board chair of Sojourners Brian McLaren writes:

> [T]here's a new kind of craziness spreading among evangelicals. It's the belief that the impossible can happen—that yes, we can stop global warming, yes, we can redirect the economy to benefit the poor majority, and yes, we can build bridges of peace instead of razor-wire-topped walls of distrust.[110]

An organization called Christian Peacemaker Teams asks and acts upon this question: what would happen if Christians devoted the same discipline and self-sacrifice to nonviolent peacemaking that armies devote to war? Motivated by a similar vision, as part of the March 16, 2007, Christian Peace Witness for Iraq, 222 ministers and laypeople engaged in nonviolent civil disobedience by praying for peace on the sidewalk in front of the White House.[111]

Some are calling this another Great Awakening, a period of dramatic religious revival in religious history similar to earlier revivals. But the change that is simultaneously taking place in other institutional structures across the spectrum makes this period of revival different from earlier ones. If religious groups join with secular groups in a common vision and a common purpose of promoting Oneness as a societal norm, the effect will be profound. This time, they have science as an ally.

Local Initiatives

Order and organizations consistent with a vision of whole-ness are percolating throughout the system at the local level. For example, some Fairfax County schools in northern Virginia are teaching peer conflict resolution to their students. The Institute of Noetic Sciences is one of a multitude of organizations whose members continually meet in local chapters to discuss and study wholeness and transformation. Small groups and organizations abound, like Boaz & Ruth, a Oneness-oriented non-profit in Richmond, Virginia, that trains the disadvantaged and those reentering society to run various businesses after being incarcerated. Meta United is one website among many devoted to positive public policy at home and abroad. Prayer circles set up by diverse groups are supporting the healing process of those who are ill. Transpartisanship invites those in politics to engage the larger whole.

As reported in Paul Hawken's book *Blessed Unrest,* there are thousands, if not hundreds of thousands, of diverse private organizations throughout the world that are striving to make the world a better place. Using the Internet to connect and cross-pollinate concepts and methodology, millions of people are helping to create a culture of Oneness.

Acceptance of Unitive Concepts

New ideas about the importance of our interconnectedness are being shared in books, videos, and film, on the Internet, and in classes at colleges and universities. For example, Dr. Masaru Emoto, in his book *The Hidden Messages in Water,* offers evidence that the vibrations of human energy, thoughts, words, ideas, and music affect the molecular structure of water. As water comprises over 70 percent of a mature human body and covers the same proportion of our planet, the implications of his experiments on how interconnected we are caught people's attention around the globe.

Conversations with God is a best-selling book about Neale Donald Walsh's mystical experiences with a higher power that developed a huge following. The DVD *The Secret,* which teaches about the power of intention in a way that would have been too New Age for the masses just a short time ago, sold millions of copies in short order. The widespread success of Eckhart Tolle's books about personal spiritual awakening, *The Power of Now* and *A New Earth,* as well as the series of Internet programs that Tolle did with television star Oprah Winfrey, reflect openness to new ideas on the part of millions of people. That openness did not exist a decade ago.

Unitive Justice

We traditionally look to the legal system for justice, but this new environment demands a holistic model of justice. Pioneers are leading the way in creating new unitive models for addressing conflict. In the area of criminal law, the old retributive system focuses on what laws were broken, who broke them, who is guilty, and who should be punished. A new model called restorative justice recognizes three key parties to crime: offender, victim, and community. To serve the needs of all three, this model is dedicated to restoration, healing, responsibility, and prevention. Restorative justice has met with a patchwork of success, in part because the distinctions between the underlying principle of Oneness and the process of duality are often not well understood or are ignored.[112] When Oneness is activated, restorative justice practices produce unitive justice.

On the civil side, a growing number of attorneys are joining the collaborative law movement. They agree that they will look for win-win solutions by putting all the facts on the table, giving advice to their clients in the presence of all parties, and empowering their clients to decide what serves them best. Among attorneys using this approach, many no longer engage in litigation. When used in a divorce, for example, collaborative law offers the benefits of being a private process that is less contentious and stressful than going to court, the outcome is likely to be much fairer because the parties are guided in finding a win-win resolution, and it models for the children a positive way for adults to work out their differences together.

As our society has become more litigious, mediation has proven to be an important structure for enhancing systemic efficiency and relieving pressure on our courts. One particular approach to mediation, called transformative mediation, sees human conflict as an opportunity to transform the conflict interaction into a positive growth experience. Through understanding, empowerment, and recognition, the parties are led to a new level of appreciation and consciousness about what has transpired and how to resolve it.[113]

New approaches to justice are by no means limited to the legal profession. Social justice refers to laypeople who are active in addressing the unfairness of laws that sustain social ills—like poverty, homelessness, and discrimination. In this model, citizens initiate the action needed to replace unjust laws and policies with holistic solutions.

These new systems represent monumental change that's quickly taking root in the central institution of law, where many of the blueprints for other institutions are made. As these unitive models of justice are experienced by a growing number of clients, victims, and offenders, this is what they will turn to at home, at school, and at work when conflicts arise. The ripple effect on our culture over time will be enormous.

Institutional Wholeness and Decay

[A]ll experience hath shewn, that mankind are more disposed to suffer, while evils are sufferable than to right themselves by abolishing the forms to which they are accustomed.
—U.S. Declaration of Independence, 1776

Although it was written in a much earlier era, the above passage from the Declaration of Independence seems just as applicable today. Discontent with the old order has been building at least since the 1960s, yet in many quarters, change has been slow in coming. Tolerance is so high because people are loath to give up what they are accustomed to. They do so only when the cost of hanging on greatly exceeds the cost of embracing change. Many of us are approaching that point.

A vision of the wholeness and the interconnectedness of all life is emerging in many institutions and disciplines. It has become a defining characteristic not only of quantum physics, but of such diverse fields as alternative and complementary medicine, biology, political science, and environmental science. The newly developed field of positive psychology measures our emotional well-being instead of our emotional illness. Agriculture is being impacted by organic farming, sustainable farming, permaculture, and biodynamic farming.

The mechanistic institutions that flourished in the recent past are being nudged aside by more holistic, inclusive structures, a process that mushroomed after the Internet enabled people from around the globe to share ideas about a better way. But institutional wholeness has only just begun.

As new structures emerge, dissatisfaction with the old order is mounting. Built on duality, it has led to pervasive chaos and disorder in the world. With its access to modern technology capable of annihilating masses of people instantly, the old order poses a threat to human survival. We now realize the old belief systems cannot lead to peace or security—they threaten our long-term existence. As though leverage is being applied to a giant fulcrum hidden from view, underlying currents we often don't notice are evidence a new order is quietly taking over.

Fifteen

A COMPASSIONATE REVOLUTION

All that keeps Oneness from being the norm
is the will of a unified people demanding that it be so.

It is time for a compassionate revolution—the melting away of fragmented duality into the all-encompassing expanse of Oneness. Many revolutions—the Protestant Reformation, the American Revolution, the French Revolution, and the Russian Revolution—have passed in history, but all have been violent, and violence is not part of the organizing principle of Oneness. Oneness will emerge, and major political and social change will occur as a natural unfolding of human evolution.

What is essential is timing. The timing of every revolution depends on a foundation of widespread discontent with the functioning of the old order, as this weakens existing structures. Under these conditions, the disequilibrium creates the conditions necessary for a handful of creative, courageous people to make a huge difference.

It is not about large numbers, favorable averages, or the latest public opinion poll, but the presence of a lone fluctuation that gets amplified by the system, a small disturbance feeding back on itself, changing and growing, with exponential effects.[114] In chaos theory it is called the phenomenon of "sensitive dependence on initial conditions." Scientists have found that, when conditions are right, a single event or series of events can trigger profound change across an entire system. This is also known as the butterfly effect.

An example of this occurred when Thomas Paine coined the phrase *the United States of America*. On January 10, 1776, Paine presented his first copy of "Common Sense" to Benjamin Franklin. It spread throughout the colonies like wildfire and, with one stroke, Paine placed the radical notion of independence at the forefront of the American debate. In their consciousness, the colonists went from being Englishmen living in a British colony at odds with the mother country over taxation, to holding the vision of being patriots living in the United States of America, politically separate and independent of England.[115]

When an entrenched system begins to break down as the English colonies did, old community beliefs give way more rapidly to new information about how to reorder the structure. When the breakdown escalates to the point that people are prepared to leave what they are familiar with and, despite their fear, try something new, the time is ripe for a transformation.

New Trends in Consciousness

Evidence that a growing number of people are ready to embrace systemic change is found in the remarkable shift in the general U.S. population that has been building for at least the last half of the twentieth century. Thirteen years of extensive research on more than one hundred thousand Americans by sociologist Paul H. Ray and psychologist Sherry Ruth Anderson found a monumental shift in U.S. culture during that time frame.

Two primary subcultures, the Traditionalists and the Modernists, had previously dominated American culture from its inception.

The modern worldview has roots in European intellectualism, in the urban merchant classes, in the rise of the modern state and armies, and in the successes of scientists and technologists. In contrast, Traditionalists place their hopes in the recovery of the small town, in religion, a nostalgic image of a time when the world was cleaner, more principled, and less conflicted, when "men were men" and authority was self-reliant. Traditionalists reject many of the so-called freedoms of modernism, from the loosening of women's roles to sexual expressiveness, and religious and ethnic inclusiveness.[116] They want a country with a set of morals that reflects their own.

But in more recent decades, Ray and Anderson report that people with a new cultural mind-set and as numerous as the population of France have quietly sprouted up in the midst of American culture.[117] They totaled about fifty million adults in the United States by the year 2000, and probably about eighty to ninety million in the European Union as well.[118]

The values of this fast-growing segment of the population are associated with wholeness; they appear to want policies that reflect our connectedness, not separation. This new subculture shares:

> serious ecological and planetary perspectives, emphasis on relationships and women's points of view, commitment to spirituality and psychological development, disaffection with the large institutions of modern life, including both left and right politics, and rejection of materialism and status display.[119]

Ray and Anderson call members of this group the Cultural Creatives, "because all across the Western world, they are literally creating a new culture."[120] They refuse to take part in the culture wars between Modernists and Traditionalists.

They head off in a third direction that's neither left nor right, neither modern nor traditional. They have been deeply involved in most of the new social movements that have appeared since the 1960s and in a host of other cultural inventions as well. Oppositional political movements have influenced them less than cultural movements that try to educate our desires and change our minds about reality. They want to see the big, inclusive picture, and they want to work with the whole system, with all the players. They regard themselves as synthesizers and healers, not just on the personal level but on the planetary level, too. They keep cutting across social class and racial lines, across ideological lines of liberal and conservative, and across national boundaries, rejecting militarism and exploitation, seeking long-term ecological sanity.[121]

At first glance, Cultural Creatives look like a typical Modernist family, but they are not. Ray and Anderson discovered that what Cultural Creatives want from life, what they see as important for the future of the country, and how they live are distinctly different from Modernists. What matters most to Cultural Creatives are issues such as our children's future, the health and education of all citizens, the ecology of the planet, the inner dimensions of life, limiting the control of big business, as well as the corrosive role of big money in politics.[122] Ray and Anderson point out that the Cultural Creatives have not yet sprung into action because they think they are an aberration, alone in their dissenting views.

The Cultural Creatives constitute but one segment of the constituency in favor of replacing old institutions founded on duality with ones that reflect Oneness. They are joined by conservative, moderate, and liberal Christians who want to return to the roots of Christ's teachings; by Muslims who see in Mohammed's teachings an all-encompassing and tolerant Allah; by Hindus and Buddhists who emphasize their ancient tradition of Oneness as the only reality; by Bahá'ís and people of other faiths whose primary religious tenets embrace Oneness; by Native Americans and aboriginal cultures who see nature as a whole system; and by scientists and secularists who embrace new theories about a unified field.

Success will depend on those who direct change, keeping a firm grasp on their intentions and not taking action prematurely, before the desire for change has ripened. They must work together and maintain links to other parts of the system. This led to the success of nonviolent movements in the 1980s that brought down dictators in the Philippines and Chile. In Poland, timing and well-maintained links enabled the workers to win the right to organize a free trade union.

If the radical—and simultaneously ancient—notion of replacing duality with Oneness were to course through our chaotic system, conditions are such that relatively few people could create the necessary fluctuation to take us to a higher order. This compassionate revolution is ready to happen.

History Points Us to the Future

How to effect regime change without war was demonstrated by the nonviolent revolution in India led by Mahatma Gandhi. Gandhi pioneered *satyagraha,* the resistance of tyranny through mass nonviolent civil disobedience, and now his birthday, October 2, is designated International Day of Nonviolence by the United Nations.

A band of young African Americans ended legal racial segregation in the United States using civil disobedience. Their weapons? Standing peacefully, with dignity, as they were spat upon, attacked by dogs, sprayed with water hoses, and clubbed by the police. In the face of such power, white southerners relinquished mass resistance and shared their public facilities.

The Truth and Reconciliation trials in South Africa restored a level of honor and peace to the nation that it could not have achieved had it sought vengeance for the political crimes committed during its years of civil strife. That nation's plan of attack? Forgiveness practiced on a wide scale. As Oneness grows stronger, you see that the power of a nation lies not in its physical might, but in the alignment of its people with love instead of fear.

Positive change occurs when committed people work for it. Consider how the role of women changed when a relatively small number of determined women demanded it. The assumption that women were incapable of civic duties has been replaced with women's right to vote, hold public office, and run for president or prime minister in a growing number of nations. Women are becoming architects, doctors, and engineers and joining many other traditionally male professions, a major change during my lifetime that opens opportunities to young women that others were once denied.

These more gentle revolutions depended upon committed leadership and willing followers. In each case, a fork in the road was taken that challenged the beliefs of many. A path was chosen that threatened the established order and caused many to feel fearful. Some were afraid that their vision of independence, integration, or liberation would fail; others feared it would succeed. What is most important is that it took few people to accomplish astonishing results, each instance adding to the impetus for a new culture of Oneness and paving the way for us.

The U.S. Role

With regard to the organizing principle of Oneness, the United States has a unique history. *E pluribus unum,* "out of many, one," is the motto of the United States adopted by the founding fathers. Consider its implications. It is a covenant that must extend to the people of all nations if it extends to any. Bahá'u'lláh, a spiritual master of the nineteenth century, provided insight in this regard when he explained the insufficiency of patriotism to one's particular nation—not that it is wrong, just incomplete in the face of the interdependence of all the peoples of the world. Love of the boundaries that separate one country from another must not be placed above love of the world, home to all of us.

For nations, the claims of humanity must supersede the claims of national interest, for seeing interests as separate is the death knell to peace and security. If, as some believe, the United States is meant to play a unique role on the world stage, surely it is that of modeling Oneness for all nations.

What can Americans do to see that the United States lives up to its motto? They can demand that the U.S. government return to being a leader in global nuclear disarmament. They can speak out for the U.S. military to be used, in concert with soldiers of other nations, to stand between the weak and those who would inflict physical harm upon them without causing more harm. They can initiate or join a discussion group examining Oneness and duality in greater detail—find others who share their concerns about the present course and who also want to be agents of change.

When the United States is called upon to intervene in another nation, the American people can insist that the work of conflict resolution and reconstruction commence immediately. This means creating a context of Oneness that empowers local citizens to become self-governing. This capacity can be built into the Department of Defense, the Department of State, or perhaps in a new Department of Peace or Department of Oneness, and be planned for well in advance. Activating Oneness will never be a job for one nation alone. By joining forces with others, the United States will show that it seeks holistic solutions and works cooperatively in the spirit of equality and the pursuit of justice for all.

Citizens can temporarily entrust their power to those who run the government day to day, but the people remain the source. Politicians may try to inject duality and fear into the process; it remains the responsibility of the citizens to curb such abuse. That is why our system depends on a well-educated, informed, and actively engaged citizenry.

By organizing at the grassroots level, Americans can use the levers of government to require their leaders to answer the needs of those in pain, as they did in Germany and Japan after World War II. Americans need not focus on their own pain, for it will heal as the healing of the whole progresses. The work of how best to organize for this new era will be the work of a new generation of U.S. legislators, policy makers, and strategists—not necessarily new in terms of length of service, but in bringing a new worldview to the task. They will be selected by a U.S. electorate determined to see the principle of Oneness prevail.

The Bridge to Oneness

Revolutions do not start at the top. Those in control will strive to cling to the old order. This gentle revolution is necessarily a grassroots movement, ready to spread from person to person and community to community. It depends on people like you and me. We must not let the magnitude of the undertaking deter us. We begin by being diligent in following the Golden Rule. When we do unto others as we would have them do unto us, we are answering the real plea our "enemies" have directed to us. We can begin now to activate Oneness, creating peace right where we are by finding the interests we share in common with others and placing our focus there.

Together we commence this compassionate revolution, one step at a time, cautiously examining where we are. Our mistakes will be used to deter us—evidence that we are misguided, that Oneness exists only as a lofty ideal, a nice Sunday sermon, but dangerous beyond that. Just as the abolitionists of slavery continued to work tirelessly, even when the obstacles appeared insurmountable, we will hold fast, the colonists and pioneers of a new world, secure in the knowledge this is now our home.

Though we stand at the threshold of new possibility, the bridge between the worlds of Oneness and duality may seem too long for us to reach the other side. Where we presently stand is the place from which to begin. Using the understanding of the organizing principle of Oneness that we now have, we can create new institutional structures. Yes, there are still those who serve as guardians of duality, who come to worship in a separated world with their old-order weapons used to keep their ancient promises of revenge. They have made their choice, but the choice for Oneness can be yours and mine—and the choice of the multitudes ready for change.

All that keeps Oneness from being the norm is the will of a unified people demanding that it be so. The old structures that are holding us back *can* be transformed so this new order can unfold. We *can* make this transformation before it's too late. The time has come for us to have faith—and to leap. We stand at a portal to the New World promised from the beginning, a promise made to ourselves that only we can keep.

Appendix

SUGGESTIONS FOR CONDUCTING DISCUSSION GROUPS

The underlying mental structures of Oneness and duality, and the institutions they give rise to, such as unitive justice and punitive justice, are thought-provoking subjects. For readers who wish to delve deeper, here are some guidelines for a discussion group facilitator, followed by suggested questions relating to each chapter.

Suggestions for the Facilitator

When a group is formed, it is important to set the context and environment *before* the discussion of content begins. First, thank everyone for attending. Acknowledge that their time is valuable and that you appreciate their caring enough to take the time to join this discussion. Second, at the first gathering you might say a few words about why you are interested in helping this discussion process take place. Third, ask everyone present to agree to a code of conduct, such as:

- One: There are no right or wrong answers within the context of this discussion. We are here to question old assumptions and to seek new insights.
- Two: We are here to understand, not persuade. We respect each person's opinion, even if we do not agree with it. Disagreement is expressed respectfully.
- Three: We agree to be honest in sharing, and to be *brief.*

- Four: If someone asks to share in confidence, everyone agrees that the identity of the person speaking will not be shared outside the group.

After reciting the four provisions, ask that everyone show consent by raising a hand. Or everyone may read the provisions out loud, then the facilitator may ask if anyone does not agree. (If someone does not agree, you might politely thank her for coming and invite her to leave in order to preserve the community spirit and cohesion, or ask her to merely observe, but not participate.) When members of the group stray from the code of conduct during the discussion, politely remind them of the agreements made in advance and that their observance is for everyone's benefit.

Create a sense of belonging to the group right from the start by asking all present to briefly introduce themselves. Ask that they state their name, why they are here, and perhaps one word or a phrase about how they feel at the moment. Ask them not to talk about roles or their profession so that the introductions serve to equalize the participants and begin to stimulate reflection.

If it is a small group, ask people to introduce themselves in turn to the entire group. If it is a large group and this would take too long, ask them to find a partner and introduce themselves to each other. Give them a set amount of time (two or three minutes total may be sufficient), and tell them when it is time to switch and when the time for introductions is up.

Participants may come with varying familiarity with the material being discussed, so be especially sensitive to those for whom it is new territory. Avoid the assumption that everyone understands the concepts or terms. Be sure to include everyone in the discussion.

If the group is large, the participants may organize into smaller groups to discuss the questions. Allow enough time for each group to make a short report back to the entire group before the discussion is adjourned. Applaud after each group report to show appreciation for their sharing.

At the conclusion, thank everyone for coming. Inform them of the time and place of the next discussion.

The length of each discussion meeting will depend on how deep your particular group would like to go. Generally, it works to explore the material in one-and-a-half-hour or two-hour segments.

To help participants become grounded in the principle of Oneness, you may design special assignments or projects to be completed in advance. For example, at the end of a discussion, you might request that participants come to the next discussion prepared to give a three-minute talk about how the principle of Oneness was reflected in something they did during the week. Or you might suggest a three-minute talk on what respect means, or how forgiveness has touched their lives.

Above all, have fun.

Suggested Discussion Questions

In addition to the questions suggested below for each chapter, you may begin each discussion with the question: in the themes presented in this chapter, what struck you as the most important or the most applicable in your life?

A suggested question to end with is: what have you heard in this discussion that you would like to take with you into the coming week?

Chapter One: Becoming Our Own Jailers

- Have you ever had any direct experience with our legal system? If so, what was the most memorable aspect of that experience?
- Do you know anyone who has spent time in jail or prison? If so, what benefit did doing time have for her? What harm did it cause to her or others?

- Have you ever judged anyone, perhaps even a child, as guilty of some wrongdoing, then discovered he was innocent? If so, what did you do to correct your mistake?
- Do you believe our criminal law system produces a value-added product? If so, what is it? If not, what should be done about it?
- Can you imagine a criminal law system that doesn't rely primarily on punitive justice? What alternatives might we consider?

Chapter Two: What Do We Mean by *Justice?*
- How do you define *justice?*
- What core beliefs support your understanding of justice? Where did you learn those core beliefs?
- When an innocent person is wrongfully incarcerated on death row for many years, what if any redress do you believe that person should have against the state? Against the prosecutor? Against the witnesses who helped convict him? Why?
- Have you been in the position where a responsibility delegated to you was in conflict with your inner moral voice? If so, how did you handle it?
- What, if anything, do you believe the Golden Rule has to do with justice?

Chapter Three: Two Forms of Justice
- Is it your responsibility to be attentive to how your lawmakers use the rule of law? If so, how can you, as a citizen, exercise such responsibility?
- Do you believe defendants who are guilty should be allowed to plead not guilty? Does your answer depend on whether it is done within a punitive system or a unitive system of justice? Why?
- Who in your life has most victimized you? What does your role as that person's victim cost you? Would forgiveness allow you more freedom?

- Do you see a relationship between punitive justice and fear? If so, how are they related?
- Are the Golden Rule and the law of an eye for an eye measures of justice that can be reconciled, one with the other? Why?

Chapter Four: The Historical Roots of Justice

- What do you believe the perfect justice system should look like? Do you believe it might be possible to achieve such a system?
- How would you describe the type of justice that you experienced most often as a child, at home, at school, or in your neighborhood? What type of justice do you most often experience now?
- Do you believe that we could have a secure nation if our legal system was based on unitive justice or lovingkindness? Why?
- How important is it that decisions made within our system of justice be based on the truth? Why? Is this possible?
- When so many of the spiritual masters over the centuries have taught us to practice lovingkindness or unitive justice, why do you believe we so infrequently do so? What is required of us for this to change?

Chapter Five: Root Causes: Oneness and Duality

- When the Amish immediately forgave the man who murdered five of their young schoolgirls in October 2006, what did you think of their response? Would you want to live like that?
- Should people who are good be held to a different moral standard from people who are the enemy or evil? What function does such dual morality serve?
- How do you define *equality*? What is the basis for your definition?
- What inequalities have you made part of your life? How much energy do you expend maintaining them?

- Can you ever attack another person without attacking or harming yourself in some way? If so, what is an example? If not, why not?

Chapter Six: Oneness: The Real Reality

- Does being hurt by another person make one a victim? What role does perception play in victimhood?
- Do games our children play teach them to believe that duality is real? That Oneness is real? Should we, as a society, care?
- Can equality be achieved on the physical level? On the spiritual level? How might spiritual equality be relevant in the physical world?
- Are there circumstances when the Golden Rule should not be applied? If so, who should decide what the exceptions are?
- Does an awareness of the distinctions between Oneness and duality help explain the conditions in our world today? If so, how?

Chapter Seven: Oneness and Religion

- Do you believe in the Source, First Cause, or God? Does this belief affect your life, and if so, how?
- If you belong to an organized religion, does it teach that God's power is all-encompassing? Does it also teach that evil is a power in its own right? If so, how are these teachings reconciled?
- Can you think of any aspect of religion that is grounded in duality and fear? If so, how did this come to be, and can it be changed to be grounded in Oneness and love?
- Did you learn the story of Adam and Eve when you were a child? If so, what underlying lessons did you take away from the story? Were there any misconceptions in what you learned?
- Do you believe that humans have a God-like nature and a fallen or sinful nature? If so, how does this belief shape your perspective on war and peace?

Chapter Eight: Science and Reality

- Does your understanding of science affect how you see the world? If so, how?
- Do you believe your thoughts influence what you experience? If so, how?
- Even though you appear separate from the people sitting next to you, do you believe you are connected to them in some unseen way? If so, how?
- What is the moral responsibility of scientists for the technology they invent? How should this responsibility be monitored or enforced?
- Do you believe human consciousness is evolving? If so, is the new science of quantum physics providing impetus to this process? How?

Chapter Nine: Oneness and the Nation-State

- Have you ever voted for a political candidate because he promised to get tough on crime? If so, what need of yours did this address? How could such needs be addressed in other ways?
- Do you see ways in which beliefs relating to our differences are used to generate fear, then to mobilize or deter action? What are some examples you have experienced?
- How might cultural assumptions about the value of punishment affect the outcome of elections? How have they done so in the past?
- How important is national identity? Can it be used in positive ways? Can it be used in negative ways?
- What are the pros and cons of more nations forming unions, as the Europeans did in forming the European Union? Would you want your country to do so, and if so, with which other nations? Why?

Chapter Ten: The Language of Oneness and Duality

- Can you give an example of judgment and an example of discernment? What is the primary difference between the two?
- If someone confronted you on a dark night brandishing a gun, do you think you could see her as innocent on some level? If so, describe what that type of innocence means.
- Does it make any difference if we confuse the terms *power* and *control?* What benefit might there be in clearly distinguishing between them?
- Have you ever forgiven someone but it was actually a conditional dispensation? If so, how did it turn out?
- What difference does it make when, in our language, we fail to distinguish between *polarity* (e.g., night and day) and *duality* (e.g., good and evil)? Does anyone benefit from this lack of clarity? Is anyone hurt by it?

Chapter Eleven: Institutionalized Oneness:
The Community Model in Corrections®

- Have you ever experienced a church, temple, mosque, or home environment that reflected some characteristics of a community model program? If so, describe that environment.
- Can you envision community model principles in institutions other than jails or prisons? If so, describe how you see this happening.
- Does your family live in a dignitarian environment, one in which the dignity of everyone is protected and honored? How is such an environment achieved?
- *Tough love* is an expression used when someone treats another person harshly with the intent of helping him in the long run. Does this lead to new insight and transformation? If so, how?
- What might be some of the reasons that the community model is not the norm in our correctional institutions? Should it be the norm?

Chapter Twelve: Institutionalized Duality: The Stanford Prison Experiment

- Have you ever experienced a work environment that reflected some characteristics of the Stanford Prison Experiment? If so, what role did you play? How did it make you feel?
- Assume you are a child who has hurt someone. Would it be easier to be punished with a spanking or by having to face the adults whom you have disappointed and the person you hurt? Why?
- Who should be held accountable for incidents like My Lai in Vietnam and for Abu Ghraib in Iraq? What should be the consequences to those who were responsible?
- What, if anything, could we as a nation have done differently after 9/11? Is there anything that we should do now in response to that event?
- Is it reasonable to offer respect to someone who has treated you with disrespect? What might be gained or lost from doing so?

Chapter Thirteen: Practicing Oneness

- Do you know anyone who has forgiven an extremely hurtful injury or violation? If so, how did this affect her life?
- Can you imagine anyone personally affected by Hitler's acts forgiving him? Is there any reason to do so?
- Do you view nonviolence (not harming others) and nonresistance (not returning the attack of those who are attacking you) differently? Is one more or less honorable than the other?
- What nonviolent means do you have available to protect yourself from being harmed by others? How effective do you believe they are?
- If the killing of humans is to be deemed moral in some circumstances, but immoral in others, who should determine where this line is drawn? Why? What if you disagree with the decision?

Chapter Fourteen: Conditions Are Ripe for Change

- Can the Internet be leveraged to facilitate change on a wide scale? Should it be used in this way? What other resources might be available for this purpose?
- Have you ever taken a course about peacemaking? If so, what did you learn that surprised you? If not, are you willing to do so?
- Where do you see your beliefs about religion or faith fitting into the principle of Oneness? Is there any need for change?
- Have you come to realize you are already involved in institutions that, in some way, are moving toward Oneness or unitive justice? If so, what form does your involvement take?
- Do you believe the old order poses a threat to our survival? What evidence supports your belief? Is change necessary or desirable?

Chapter Fifteen: A Compassionate Revolution

- What segment of the culture are you a part of: Traditionalists, Modernists, Cultural Creatives, or something else? What difference does this make in how you view Oneness and duality?
- Do you believe it is possible that millions of people are ready to embrace the transition from duality to Oneness? If so, what do you think is needed to mobilize them into coordinated action?
- Are you interested in making the transition from duality to Oneness? If so, what will be your next step toward this goal? If not, why not?
- Is there someone you need to forgive in order to experience Oneness yourself? If so, are you willing to do so?
- Do we stand in a pivotal moment in history? If so, how can you seize this moment and use it for transformation?

Notes

1. My seeing law and other institutions differently began to accelerate when I first read *A Course in Miracles* in 1987.

2. Pew Center on the States, *One in 100: Behind Bars in America 2008,* February 28, 2008, 3, http://www.pewcenteronthestates.org/uploadedFiles/8015PCTS_Prison08_FINAL_2-1-1_FORWEB.pdf. Unless otherwise stated, all incarceration statistics in this chapter are from this report.

3. The term *incarceration binge* may have been coined by James Austin et al., "Unlocking America: Why and How to Reduce America's Prison Population," The JFA Institute (2007), http://www.pretrial.org/Docs/Documents/UnlockingAmerica.pdf. That is the first place I read it.

4. Adam Liptak, "1 in 100 U.S. Adults Behind Bars, New Study Says," *New York Times,* February 28, 2008, http://www.nytimes.com/2008/02/28/us/28cnd-prison.html?_r=1&hp=&oref=slogin&pagewanted=print.

5. Amanda Petteruti and Nastassia Walsh, *Jailing Communities: The Impact of Jail Expansion and Effective Public Safety Strategies,* Justice Policy Institute (April 2008), 3, http://www.justicepolicy.org/images/upload/0804_REP_JailingCommunities_AC.pdf.

6. Pew Center on the States, *One in 31: The Long Reach of American Corrections* (March 2009), 12, http://www.pewcenteronthestates.org/uploadedFiles/PSPP_1in31_report_FINAL_WEB_3-26-09.pdf.

7. Michael Wines, "Ideas and Trends: After 30 Years; Mental Institutions May Be as Empty as They'll Ever Be," *New York Times,* September 4, 1988, http://query.nytimes.com/gst/fullpage.html?res=940DEEDD1F3AF937A3575AC0A96E948260&sec=&spon=&pagewanted=1.

8. Petteruti and Walsh, 9. See also PBS *Frontline,* www.pbs.org/wgbh/pages/frontline/shows/asylums.

9. Deborah J. Vagins and Jesselyn McCurdy, *Cracks in the System: Twenty Years of the Unjust Federal Crack Cocaine Law,* American Civil Liberties Union (October 2006), ii. A few weeks after Bias's death, Congress passed the Anti-Drug Abuse Act of 1986. This established mandatory minimum sentences for specific quantities of cocaine.

[10]Pew Center on the States, *One in 100,* 12.

[11]Pew Center on the States, *One in 100,* 12–13.

[12]James Austin and Tony Fabelo, "The Diminishing Returns of Increased Incarceration," JFA Institute (2004), 2, http://www.jfa-associates.com/BlueprintFinal.pdf.

[13]Pew Center on the States, "Pew Report Finds More Than One in 100 Adults Are Behind Bars," press release, February 28, 2008, http://www.pewcenteronthestates.org/news_room_detail.aspx?id=35912.

[14]Justice Policy Institute, *The Punishing Decade: Prison and Jail Estimates at the Millennium* (May 2000), 4, http://www.justicepolicy.org/images/upload/00-05_REP_PunishingDecade_AC.pdf.

[15]Petteruti and Walsh, 8.

[16]Austin et al., "Unlocking America," 4.

[17]Pew Center on the States, "Pew Report."

[18]Kimberly Fauss, a collaborative law attorney with expertise in neuropsychology, describes how this process unfolds in a typical divorce. "The husband tells his story, with the assistance of his highly-trained lawyer, which focuses on all the negative events from the shared past of the family. The positive, happy memories are ignored in order to develop the best case for some current objective. By formalizing this 'story,' which is told from only one perspective in an official setting, the 'victim and villain' mentality is set and hardened into neural networks. The wife likewise retells past events from another perspective and both begin the legal discovery process of validating their own story with carefully selected evidence. Throughout the year or more usually required to obtain a final divorce, this painful, negative story may well be locked into the long-term memory of the hippocampus. A new perspective is not created, but rather the court chooses one story over the other in a win-lose ending." Kimberly P. Fauss, "Collaborative Professionals as Healers of Conflict: The Conscious Use of Neuroscience in Collaboration," *Collaborative Review* 10:2 (Summer 2008), 1.

[19]Studies indicate that there is a positive correlation between children from divorced homes and higher rates of delinquency (status offenses, crimes against persons, felony theft, general delinquency, tobacco and drug use except alcohol use) when compared to children from intact homes. Cynthia Price and Jenifer Kunz, "Rethinking the Paradigm of Juvenile Delinquency as Related to Divorce," *Journal of Divorce & Remarriage* 39:1–2 (September 1, 2003), 125–127.

[20]Death Penalty Information Center, "Exonerations by State," http://www.deathpenaltyinfo.org/innocence-and-death-penalty#inn-st.

[21]Tim Carpenter, "Ex-prosecutor: 'I made a mistake,'" *The Topeka Capital Journal,* http://cjonline.com/news/legislature/2009-11-14/ex_prosecutor_i_made_a_ mistake, cited November 15, 2009.

[22]A 1991 Johns Hopkins University study found lawyers experienced more depression than any other profession. While up to 10 percent of U.S. adults chronically abuse alcohol, for attorneys the rate is 25 percent, increasing with time in the profession. Glen Mirando, "Lawyers: Are We a Profession in Distress?" *Ethics Online,* Oklahoma Bar Association (2009), http://www.okbar.org/ethics /mirando.htm#2.

[23]Coe Swobe, "Lawyers Concerned for Lawyers," *State Bar of Nevada,* April 1, 2002, http://www.nvbar.org/nevadalawyerarticles3.asp?Title=Lawyers+Conce rned+for+Lawyers. The article states, "[S]tatistical data suggests that lawyers are more at risk for suicide than any other profession or vocation. In recent years, the State Bar of Nevada experienced six suicides in four years."

[24]Some may question how unitive justice differs from restorative justice. Restorative justice can be the same as unitive justice, but I have chosen to use a new term because some authorities in the restorative justice movement believe it is desirable to employ guilt and shame to achieve compliance. *See,* for example, John Braithwaite, *Crime, Shame and Reintegration* (Cambridge: Cambridge University Press, 1989), 1–15. As I will discuss later in the book, guilt and shame are related to duality, and are inconsistent with Oneness. Unitive justice is achieved when the justice being implemented is fully consistent with the principles of Oneness, thus guilt and shame cannot be a part of it.

[25]Torah, Hosea 6:6.

[26]Obery M. Hendricks Jr., *The Politics of Jesus: Rediscovering the True Revolutionary Nature of Jesus' Teachings and How They Have Been Corrupted* (New York: Doubleday, 2006), 111–112.

[27]Bible, Leviticus 24:19–20.

[28]*Encyclopædia Britannica* "Code of Hammurabi," (2009), http://www.britannica .com/EBchecked/topic/253710/Code-of-Hammurabi.

[29]Department of History, "Communal Courts," University of Houston, http:// vi.uh.edu/pages/bob/elhone/comcrts.html.

[30]In some of the early Eastern cultures, the wisdom Jesus taught had long been known. Buddha did not advise attack; he taught compassion and mindfulness. Some even hypothesize that the teachings of Jesus may have had their roots in Eastern philosophy.

[31] *Lovingkindness* is the term used in the King James Version of the Bible to translate the Jewish term *hesed*. As discussed in chapter 4, *hesed* is the unitive form of justice referenced in the Old Testament, in contrast to *mishpat*, the punitive form of justice.

[32] Bible, John 13:34.

[33] John Allen and Desmond Tutu, *The Essential Desmond Tutu* (South Africa: Mayibuye Books, 1997), 7.

[34] Tanakh, Nevi'im, Isaiah 45:22.

[35] Tanakh, Torah, Exodus 3:14.

[36] Bible, Mark 12:28–29.

[37] Bible, Matthew 5:17.

[38] Bible, Acts 17:28.

[39] Bible, Genesis 2:17.

[40] Bible, Genesis 2:21.

[41] The Sanskrit term, *dhárma* (*dhamma* in Pali), is an Indian spiritual and religious term that means one's righteous duty or virtuous path.

[42] Bible, Genesis 1:26.

[43] David Bohm, *Wholeness and the Implicate Order* (Padstow, Eng.: T. J. Press, 1980), 8–9.

[44] Bohm, 16.

[45] David Osborne and Peter Plastrik, *Banishing Bureaucracy: The Five Strategies for Reinventing Government* (Reading, Mass.: Addison-Wesley Publishing, 1998), 16.

[46] Bohm, 9.

[47] Bohm, 9.

[48] Fred Alan Wolf, *The Dreaming Universe: A Mind-Expanding Journey into the Realm Where Psyche and Physics Meet* (New York: Touchstone, 1994), 348–349.

[49] CNN.com, "Poll: Bin Laden Tops Musharraf in Pakistan," Terror Free Tomorrow (September 11, 2007), 1–2, http://www.terrorfreetomorrow.org/upimagestft/CNN%20Story.pdf.

[50] CNN.com, 2.

[51] *The Fog of War: Eleven Lessons from the Life of Robert S. McNamara,* directed by Errol Morris (2003).

[52] *The Fog of War.*

[53]Benjamin H. Friedman, *Opinion: The U.S. Should Cut Military Spending in Half* (Christian Science Monitor, April 27, 2009), http://www.csmonitor .com/2009/0427/p09s01-coop.html, cited November 17, 2009. (Friedman is a research fellow in defense and homeland security studies at the Cato Institute and a PhD candidate in political science at MIT.)

[54]Chalmers Johnson, *The Sorrows of Empire: Militarism, Secrecy, and the End of the Republic* (New York: Metropolitan Books, 2004), 64.

[55]Andrew J. Bacevich, *The New American Militarism: How Americans Are Seduced by War* (New York: Oxford University Press, 2005), 1.

[56]Chalmers Johnson, 1.

[57]U.S. Department of Justice, Bureau of Justice Statistics (June 1994). "Prisoners in 1993." Washington D.C.: 13, Table 18, cited by Tara-Jen Ambrosio and Vincent Schiraldi, *From Classrooms to Cell Blocks: A National Perspective,* Justice Policy Institute (February 1997), http://www.justicepolicy.org/images/upload/97-01_REP_ ClassroomsCellblocksNational_BB.pdf.

[58]Austin et al., "Unlocking America," 1.

[59]Joe McGinniss, *The Selling of the President: The Classic Account of Packaging of a Candidate* (New York: Penguin Books, 1988), xv–xvi.

[60]McGinniss, 11–12.

[61]Justice Policy Institute, "The Punishing Decade: Prison and Jail Estimates at the Millennium" (May 2000), 1, http://www.justicepolicy.org/images/up-load/00-05_REP_PunishingDecade_AC.pdf.

[62]The Sentencing Project, "New Incarceration Figures: Thirty-three Consecutive Years of Growth" (December 2006), 1, http://www.sentencingproject.org /Admin/Documents/publications/inc_newfigures.pdf.

[63]Karl Menninger, MD, *The Crime of Punishment* (New York: Viking Press, 1966), 251–252.

[64]James Turner Johnson, *Just War Tradition and the Restraint of War: A Moral and Historical Inquiry* (Princeton, N.J.: Princeton University Press, 1981), 121.

[65]James Turner Johnson, 123.

[66]Community Model in Corrections® is a program developed for correctional facilities by Morgan Moss, Ed.S., who has been working in corrections for more than twenty years, and Penny Patton, Ed.S., who has been working in corrections for more than a decade. They are also the codirectors of the Center for Thera-

peutic Justice. Their work was featured in the September/October 2003 and the January/February 2006 issues of *American Jails* magazine.

[67]Penny B. Patton, "Community Model" (CFTJ paper, 2007).

[68]Rudi Schuster.

[69]Robert W. Fuller, *All Rise: Somebodies, Nobodies, and the Politics of Dignity* (San Francisco: Berrett-Khoeler Publishers, 2006).

[70]V. Morgan Moss Jr., "Changing the Culture of Incarceration," *American Jails* (September–October 2003), 17.

[71]Addicts become masters at first-order change, as it is needed to survive and at the same time sustain their addiction. It is also prevalent in businesses, organizations, and government institutions where hierarchy and control is strictly enforced.

[72]In other settings, this model is sometimes called "self-organizing learning" or "self-help/mutual aid."

[73]This study was conducted by the Virginia Department of Criminal Justice Services under the direction of Rudi Schuster.

[74]Bureau of Justice Statistics, "Reentry Trends in the U.S.: Recidivism," U.S. Department of Justice, at http://www.ojp.usdoj.gov/bjs/reentry/recidivism.htm, cited November 20, 2009.

[75]David R. Hawkins, *I: Relativity and Subjectivity* (West Sedona, Ariz.: Veritas Publishing, 2003), xxvi.

[76]Hawkins.

[77]For more information, see the official website at http://www.dhamma.org.

[78]Produced by Jenny Phillips, http://www.dhammabrothers.com/.

[79]Philip Zimbardo, *The Lucifer Effect: Understanding How Good People Turn Evil* (New York: Random House, 2008), 33.

[80]*Quiet Rage: The Stanford Prison Experiment,* directed by Philip G. Zimbardo (2007).

[81]*Quite Rage.*

[82]Zimbardo, 223.

[83]Zimbardo, 226.

[84]Zimbardo, 226.

[85]Laurie Meyers, "Evil's Mundane Roots," *Monitor on Psychology* 38:9 (October 2007), 21.

86Zimbardo, 450.

87President George W. Bush, address to APEC (Lima, Peru, November 22, 2008), http://georgewbush-whitehouse.archives.gov/news/releases/2008/11/20081122-7.html.

88President George W. Bush, speech at the Pentagon (Washington, D.C., September 17, 2001), http://www.nytimes.com/2001/09/18/us/excerpts-from-bush-s-remarks-on-retaliation.html.

89Francis Fukuyama, *America at the Crossroads: Democracy, Power and the Neoconservative Legacy* (New Haven and London: Yale University Press, 2007), 156.

90Michael R. Gordon, "After Hard-Won Lessons, Army Doctrine Revised," *New York Times,* February 8, 2008), http://www.nytimes.com/2008/02/08/washington/08strategy.html?_r=1&hp=&oref=slogin&pagewanted=print.

91This is a common affirmative defense available to defendants. The accused has the burden of persuading the fact finder that he acted in defense of self or another to the degree necessary to raise a reasonable doubt about his guilt. *See,* for example, *Lynn v. Commonwealth of Virginia,* 499 S.E.2d 1, 27 Va. App. 336 (1998).

92*See* http://www.sfheart.com/Gandhi.html.

93Swami Prabhavananda, *The Sermon on the Mount According to Vedanta* (Hollywood, Calif.: Vedanta Press, 1992), 58–61.

94*The Tao of Power: Lao Tsu's Classic Guide to Leadership, Influence, and Excellence*, translated by R. L. Wing (New York: Random House, 1986), 68.

95Lord Chalmers, *Dialogues of the Buddha* (London: Oxford University Press, 1926), http://www.archive.org/stream/bookofdiscipline05hornuoft/bookofdiscipline05hornuoft_djvu.txt.

96Bible (Living), Matthew 5:39–48.

97Glenda Green, *Love Without End: Jesus Speaks* (Sedona, Ariz: Spirits Publishing, 2002), 52.

98The United Nations reports that the number of older persons (over sixty) in the world has tripled over the last fifty years, and it will more than triple again over the next fifty years. Department of Economic and Social Affairs, Population Division, *World Population Ageing: 1950–2050,* United Nations (2002), 11, http://www.un.org/esa/population/publications/worldageing19502050/.

99The diminishing importance of humans in production has been compared to the diminished role of horses when tractors were introduced into farming.

[100]According to insurance statistics as of 2001, the frequency of major natural disasters is now three times what it was in the 1960s. Bernard Lietaer, *The Future of Money: Creating New Wealth, Work and a Wiser World*, (London: Century, 2001), 13.

[101]As what happens in one part of the world is no longer isolated in its effects, economists are finding a global economy poses greater problems than had been expected. Problems that were thought to be curable are too often intractable. *See* Lietaer, 15–16.

[102]Peter Russell, *The White Hole in Time: Our Future Evolution and the Meaning of Now* (San Francisco: HarperSanFrancisco, 1992), 198.

[103]Anthony M. Townsend, "The Science of Location: Why the Wireless Development Community Needs Geography, Urban Planning and Architecture" (position paper submitted for CHI 2001 Wireless Workshop), 3.

[104]For more information, see http://www.regenerativedesign.org/.

[105]Patricia Aburdene, *Megatrends 2010: The Rise of Conscious Capitalism* (Charlottesville, Va.: Hampton Roads, 2007), xvi.

[106]Lietaer, 7–8.

[107]*See* Peter A. Hall and David Soskice, eds., *Varities of Capitalism: The Institutional Foundations of Comparative Advantage* (Oxford: Oxford University Press, 2001).

[108]Jim Wallis, *The Great Awakening: Reviving Faith and Politics in a Post-Religious Right America* (New York: HarperCollins, 2008).

[109]Nicholas D. Kristof, "Evangelicals a Liberal Can Love," *New York Times* (February 3, 2008), http://www.nytimes.com/2008/02/03/opinion/03kristof.html?_r=1&th=&oref=slogin&emc=th&pagewanted=print.

[110]Brian McLaren, "Crazy Evangelicals," *God's Politics* blog (February 5, 2008), http://blog.beliefnet.com/godspolitics/2008/02/crazy-evangelicals-by-brian-mc.html.

[111]"Civil disobedience scenario," *Christian Peace Witness Newsletter* (February 10, 2008).

[112]For an in-depth report on costs and recidivism rates in various types of restorative programs, such as victim-offender mediation, group conferencing, and circles, see M. S. Umbreit, B. Vos, and R. B. Coates, "Restorative Justice Dialogue: Evidence-Based Practice," University of Minnesota School of Social Work, Center for Restorative Justice and Peacemaking (January 1, 2006), http://www.cehd.umn.edu/ssw/rjp/PDFs/RJ_Dialogue_Evidence-based_Practice_1-06.pdf.

[113]Robert A. Baruch Bush and Joseph P. Folger, *The Promise of Mediation: The Transformative Approach to Conflict* (San Francisco: John Wiley, 2005), 18–19.

[114]Margaret J. Wheatley, *Leadership and the New Science: Learning About Organizations from an Orderly Universe* (San Francisco: Berrett-Koehler Publishers, 1992), 95–96.

[115]Joseph Sohm, "1776: The American Evolution," *Perspectives* 6:4 (August 22, 2001), 2.

[116]Paul H. Ray and Sherry Ruth Anderson, *The Cultural Creatives: How 50 Million People Are Changing the World* (New York: Harmony, 2000), 80.

[117]Ray and Anderson, 3.

[118]Cultural Creatives, http://www.culturalcreatives.org/.

[119]Ray and Anderson, 4.

[120]Paul H. Ray, *The New Political Compass* (2002), 23, http://www.spiraldynamics.org/documents/NewPoliticalCompassV7.3.pdf.

[121]Ray and Anderson, 94.

[122]Ray, 6.

Postscript

The writing of this book was, in large part, a collective effort. It began in 2007 with the first drafts edited by Deborah Woodward, who provided support and guidance in addition to professional editing. Those early drafts were then discussed by small focus groups and later by an ongoing discussion group that met over the course of several months. The next step was for individuals to review the evolving manuscript and give me feedback, a process that took over two years. Special thanks to Hampton Roads editor Randy Davila who believed in this book from the beginning, and to copyeditors Ali McCart and Rachel Leach.

My gratitude to everyone who was involved in this creative process: Donna Pendarvis, Sarah Knorr, Nancy Cook, Kay Holmes, Bob Holmes, Michelle Kirby, Matt Sexstone, Ned Campbell, Kathi Campbell, Brenda French, Brandy Bollinger, Vanessa Kinlaw, Louise Strait, Susanne Shilling, Josie Sicheri, Julie M. Sulik, Steven Roth, Gena Borda, Shafia Eve, Kimberly King, Anne Davis, John Fair, Thomas Ann Hines, Jack Kloenne, Alice Dansker Doyle, Mike Hendrickson, Margaret DuVall, Jane-Marie Gilbert, Ann Larabee, Morgan Moss, Penny Patton, Ray Tademy, Malik Khan, Hugh Eckert, Dwight Smith, Marianne Pearce, Patricia Johnson, Jacqueline Pogue, Marvin Vining, Ray Rust, Stase Michaels, Laura Fox, Suzanne Starseed, Christa Pierpont, Jim Mustin, Brian Vaughn, Lorraine Cook, and John Price.

Integral to the process were also my husband, Eric Johnson, and our children, Andrea, Weston, and Danielle. Our grandchildren, Sam, Mae, and Laina, made it all worthwhile.

About the Author

Sylvia Clute is a former trial attorney. She holds an MA in Pubic Administration from the Harvard Kennedy School of Government, a Juris Doctor from Boston University School of Law, and an MA in Public Administration from the University of California at Berkeley. After graduating from law school and establishing a practice, Clute co-founded the only women's bank in the South, became chairman of the board, and helped move Virginia's laws relating to women and children into the twentieth century. She is currently president of the Restorative Justice Association of Virginia. She lives with her family in Richmond, Virginia.